What economic forces shape the development and adoption of new technologies? How do funding decisions, institutional contexts, and market structures influence which innovations succeed and which fail? What are the broader societal consequences of technological change?

The books in this series examine the economic and organizational dynamics that drive technological innovation. The series editor, Albert N. Link, welcomes book proposals from researchers investigating how technologies are conceived, financed, developed, and brought to market, as well as how they diffuse across sectors and societies. Such books might provide analyses using project-, firm-, industry-, agency-, or national-level data; comparative or longitudinal studies; and evaluations of the returns on public and private investment in innovation. The series is particularly focused on work that connects micro-level mechanisms with macro-level outcomes, offering insight into the interplay between technological advancement, economic performance, and social transformation.

All proposals submitted to the series undergo single-blind peer review by subject-matter experts prior to acceptance. Completed manuscripts are evaluated by the series editor or an assigned expert before production can begin.

Albert N. Link · Alan C. O'Connor

The Economics of Heart Disease Research

Knowledge Transfers, Funding, and US National Institutes of Health

palgrave
macmillan

Albert N. Link
Department of Economics
University of North Carolina at Greensboro
Greensboro, NC, USA

Alan C. O'Connor
RTI International
Research Triangle Park, NC, USA

ISSN 2662-3862 ISSN 2662-3870 (electronic)
Palgrave Advances in the Economics of Innovation and Technology
ISBN 978-3-032-13546-9 ISBN 978-3-032-13547-6 (eBook)
https://doi.org/10.1007/978-3-032-13547-6

This Palgrave Macmillan imprint is published by the registered company Springer Nature Switzerland AG.
The registered company address is: Gewerbestrasse 11, 6330 Cham, Switzerland

For our beloved families

Acknowledgements Many thanks to those at the National Research Council within the US National Academies of Sciences, Engineering, and Medicine for making available to us the Small Business Innovation Research (SBIR) data considered in this book.

We are also grateful to our many colleagues at the University of North Carolina at Greensboro and at RTI International for their comments and suggestions on numerous earlier drafts of this book. Thanks too to anonymous reviewers who graciously shared their suggestions for revisions of our original manuscript. Their effort improved our presentation of our thoughts in this book.

A special thank you to Ms. Bronwyn Geyer, Commissioning Editor at Palgrave Macmillan, for her editorial guidance. Thanks too to Anand Manimudichozhan, Production Editor at Palgrave Macmillan, for shepherding this book through the production process at Palgrave Macmillan.

Competing Interests The authors have no competing interests to declare that are relevant to the content of this manuscript.

Contents

About the Authors

Albert N. Link is Professor Emeritus, Department of Economics, at the University of North Carolina at Greensboro (UNCG) and Senior Research Fellow at the Institute for Development Strategies at Indiana University Bloomington O'Neill School of Public and Environmental Affairs. Prior to retirement, Link was the Virginia Batte Phillips Distinguished Professor at UNCG.

Link received the B.S. degree in mathematics from the University of Richmond (Phi Beta Kappa) and the Ph.D. degree in economics from Tulane University.

Link's research focuses on technology and innovation policy, the economics of R&D, and policy evaluation. He is the Editor-in-Chief of the *Journal of Technology Transfer*. He is also co-editor of *Foundations and Trends in Entrepreneurship*, and founder and editor of *Annals of Science and Technology Policy*.

Link is author/co-author or editor/co-editor of more than 70 books. His other research consists of more than 250 authored/co-authored peer-reviewed journal articles and book chapters as well as numerous US government reports.

Link's public service includes being a member of the National Research Council's research team that conducted the 2010 evaluation of the US Small Business Innovation Research (SBIR) program. Based on that assignment, he testified before the US Congress in April 2011 on the economic benefits associated with the SBIR program. Link also served from 2007 to 2012 as the US Representative to the United Nations (Geneva, Switzerland) in the capacity of co-vice chairperson of the Team of Specialists on Innovation and Competitiveness Policies Initiative for the Economic Commission for Europe. In October 2018, he delivered the European Commission Distinguished Scholar Lecture at the European Commission's Joint Research Centre.

Alan C. O'Connor is Senior Vice President for Environment and Senior Economist in the Center for Applied Economics and Strategy at RTI International. He received the B.A. degree in economics and political science from the University of North Carolina at Chapel Hill, and the MBA degree from the Middlebury Institute of International Studies at Monterey.

O'Connor has 25 years of experience in R&D policy and programs, academic entrepreneurship, economic development, and research impact assessment. His core practice consists of program evaluations, benefit-cost analyses, retrospective and prospective social return on investment studies, and program strategy and learning. He has significant experience with small businesses and translational science programs funded by national government agencies, including the National Institutes of Health. He has evaluated the impact of several SBIR/STTR portfolios as well as proof-of-concept programs, such as the NIH Centers for Accelerated Innovation and the Research Evaluation and Commercialization Hubs programs.

O'Connor is co-author of *Battery Technology for Electric Vehicles: Public Science and Private Innovation* (Routledge, 2015), co-author of *Public Investments in Energy Technology* (Edward Elgar, 2012), and co-author of numerous domestic and international government reports. His scholarship has also appeared in such journals as *Science and Public Policy, Small Business Economics, The Journal of Technology Transfer, Annals of Science and Technology Policy, Annals of the New York Academy of Sciences, Vaccine, The American Journal of Managed Care*, and *Economics of Innovation and New Technology.*

O'Connor is globally regarded as an expert on program evaluation methodology and methods; he consults internationally through RTI International.

List of Abbreviations

CDC	Center for Disease Control
CRADA	Cooperative Research and Development Agreement
CRP	Commercialization Readiness Pilot program
CRS	Congressional Research Service
CVD	Cardiovascular Disease
DOC	Department of Commerce
DOD	Department of Defense
DOE	Department of Energy
DHS	Department of Homeland Security
DOT	Department of Transportation
EC	European Commission
ED	Department of Education
EPA	Environmental Protection Agency
FY	Fiscal Year
GDP	Gross Domestic Product
HHS	Department of Health and Human Services
HLBS	Heart, Lung, Blood, and Sleep Health
IP	Intellectual Property
KT	Knowledge Transfer
NASA	National Aeronautics and Space Administration
NCI	National Cancer Institute
NBER	National Bureau of Economic Research
NEI	National Eye Institute
NHI	National Hearth Institute
NHLI	National Heart and Lung Institute
NIH	National Institute/Institutes of Health
NHLBI	National Heart, Lung, and Blood Institute

NHGRI	National Human Genome Research Institute
NIA	National Institute on Aging
NIAAA	National Institute on Alcohol Abuse and Alcoholism
NIAID	National Institute of Allergy and Infectious Diseases
NIAMS	National Institute of Arthritis and Musculoskeletal and Skin Diseases
NIBIB	National Institute of Biomedical Imaging and Bioengineering
NICHD	National Institute of Child Health and Human Development
NIDCD	National Institute on Deafness and other Communication Disorders
NIDCR	National Institute of Dental and Craniofacial Research
NIDDK	National Institute of Diabetes and Digestive and Kidney Diseases
NIDA	National Institute on Drug Abuse
NIEHS	National Institute of Environmental Health Sciences
NIGMS	National Institute of General Medical Sciences
NIMH	National Institute of Mental Health
NIMHD	National Institute of Minority Health and Health Disparities
NINDS	National Institute of Neurological Disorders and Stroke
NINR	National Institute of Nursing Research
NIST	National Institute of Standards and Technology
NLM	National Library of Medicine
NRC	National Research Council
NSF	National Science Foundation
OECD	Organisation for Economic Co-operation and Development
PHS	Public Health Service
PRO	Publicly Funded Research Organization
R&D	Research and Development
S&E	Science and Engineering
SBA	Small Business Administration
SBIR	Small Business Innovation Research
SDB	Socially and Economically Disadvantaged Business
SEED	Small Business Education and Entrepreneurial Development
STTR	Small Business Technology Transfer
TM	Third Mission
TPO	Technology Partnerships Office
US	United States
U.S.C.	United States Code
USDA	United States Department of Agriculture
USPTO	United States Patent and Trademark Office
WHO	World Health Organization
WOSB	Woman-Owned Small Business

List of Figures

List of Tables

CHAPTER 1

Introduction: US Trends in Heart Disease

Abstract In the United States, heart disease is the leading cause of death. The National Heart, Lung, and Blood Institute (NHLBI) within the National Institutes of Health (NIH) leads the nation in the sponsorship of heart disease research. The chapters in this book, which are summarized in this introductory chapter, describe the economics of NHLBI's support of heart disease research with a focus on the transfer into society of the scientific knowledge that has emanated from the Institute's funded research projects. Examples of such research projects are included in this chapter.

In the United States, based on 2024 information from the Center for Disease Control (CDC): "Heart disease is the leading cause of death for men, women, and people of most racial and ethnic groups."[1] And similarly, the World Health Organization (WHO) previously wrote, based on 2019 data, that: "Cardiovascular diseases (CVDs) are the leading cause of death globally, taking an estimated 17.9 million lives each year."[2] From an international perspective, among OECD (Organisation for Economic Co-operation and Development) countries, the death rate per 100,000 in the

[1] See https://www.cdc.gov/heart-disease/data-research/facts-stats/index.html.

[2] See https://www.who.int/health-topics/cardiovascular-diseases#tab=tab_1.

A. N. Link, A. C. O'Connor, *The Economics of Heart Disease Research*, Palgrave Advances in the Economics of Innovation and Technology, https://doi.org/10.1007/978-3-032-13547-6_1

United States was 114.3 in 2021. In 2021, in Germany it was 102.4, in the United Kingdom it was 83.8, in Canada it was 80.2, and in Switzerland it was 58.4.

Regarding the trend in heart-related deaths in the United States, cardiovascular disease (CVD) mortality decreased from 2010 through 2019, but it increased during the initial years of the Covid-19 pandemic (2020 to 2022). It is uncertain whether that trend will increase (Woodruff et al., 2024).

Another US trend to consider is the percentage of total deaths in the country that are due to heart disease. The Institute for Health Metrics and Evaluation reports that in 1990 the percent of US deaths due to ischemic[3] heart disease was 27.74%, but in 2021 the percent had decreased to 14.21%.[4] See Fig. 1.1. Still, heart disease remains as the number one cause of death in the United States.

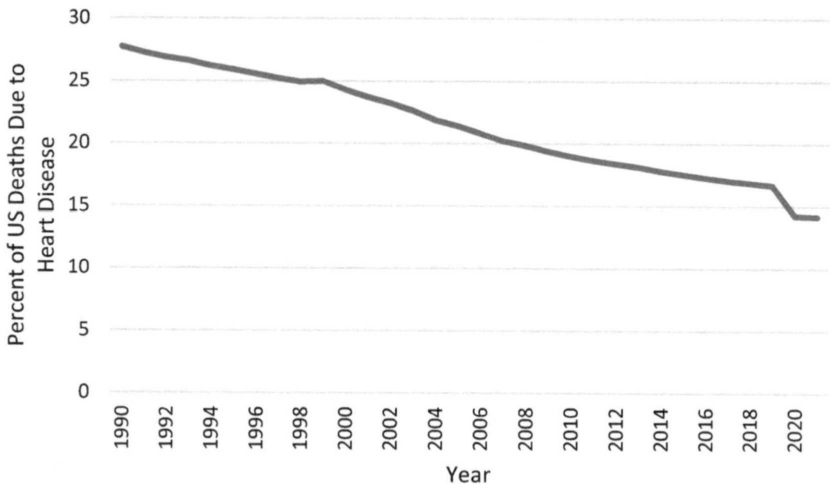

Fig. 1.1 Percent of US Deaths Due to Heart Disease, 1990–2021. *Source* https://vizhub.Healthdata.Org/gbd-compare/

[3] Ischemia refers to reduced blood flow from the heart to other parts of one's body.

[4] See https://vizhub.healthdata.org/gbd-compare/.

In the United States, the National Heart, Lung, and Blood Institute (NHLBI) within the National Institutes of Health (NIH), within the Department of Health and Human Services (HHS), has led the nation in heart disease research.[5]

> For more than 60 years, the NHLBI has led the fight against heart and vascular diseases. The NHLBI supports research to advance the understanding of and interventions for pediatric and adult heart and vascular diseases, including heart attack, heart failure, stroke, and congenital heart disease. Over this period, steady, long-term investments in biomedical research have contributed to a 71 percent decrease in death rates due to coronary heart disease, yet more remains to be done. Heart disease is still the leading cause of death for men and women. The NHLBI has a long history of groundbreaking research in treatments for high blood pressure, a common condition that increases the risk for heart disease and stroke, two of the leading causes of death for Americans.

The NHLBI, which by legislation allocates 3% of its extramural budget to support small businesses, is not alone in its funded research focused on reducing deaths from heart disease. In the United Kingdom, there is the Medical Research Council; in Australia, there is the National Institutes of Health; and in Canada, there is the Canadian Institutes of Health Research. However, the NHLBI's support of research by small firms is, to the best of our knowledge, unparalleled around the world.

Medical journals and medical texts aside, there is a conspicuous void of scholarly inquiry about the economics of heart disease research and about the public policy initiatives that fund the related research, especially in small firms. This book represents an important first step forward for medically trained professionals (e.g., physicians and administrators) as well as those who are not non-medically trained (e.g., economists, policy scientists, and legislators) but are interested to learn about the small firm research activities supported by the NHLBI and about the economic and policy implications of the research that this Institute supports. And, to the best of our knowledge, this book is the first systematic effort to focus on NHLBI as an Institute within the NIH. Equally unique is our emphasis on scientific knowledge and innovative activity in small firms that was funded through the NHLBI programs.

[5] See https://www.nhlbi.nih.gov/science/heart-and-vascular-diseases.

Our approach in this book to describe the economics of NHLBI's support of heart disease research is to focus on the transfer into society of the scientific knowledge that has emanated from the research projects of small firms that were funded by the NHLBI. This approach allows us to segue from a description of socially important knowledge transfers to public policy initiatives to enhance such socially important research.

As context, Table 1.1 provides abstracts from selected recent NHLBI-funded projects that were related directly to heart disease. These projects were funded through the NHLBI Small Business Innovation Research (SBIR) program (discussed in Chap. 3). While these abstracts are quoted directly from funded firms' descriptions of their research, and are thus technical in scope, they nevertheless provide context as well as insight into the breadth of health disease research in small firms funded by the NHLBI.

Small firms are, of course, only one segment of the research population involved in heart disease research. Other segments include universities and large research-based entities. Our choice to focus on small firms is pragmatic; we have access to a unique data set from which we can glean the relationship between research award amounts and the knowledge transfer performance of the funded small firms. Again, to the best of our knowledge, this is the first systematic effort to focus exclusively and in detail on NHLBI's SBIR program from an economic perspective and the performance of firms funded through that program. Thus, the remainder of this book is organized as follows.

Chapter 2 introduces the concept of knowledge transfers because they are the metric through which we quantify the performance of small NHLBI-funded firms. The term *knowledge transfer* is more common in the European Union than in the United States. The policy importance of knowledge transfers was recently popularized through the publication of a European Commission report entitled *Knowledge Transfer Metrics: Towards a European-Wide Set of Harmonized Indicators*. In the United States, a more commonly used term is *technology transfer* rather than *knowledge transfer*. Technology transfer metrics are a subset of knowledge transfer metrics. Both knowledge and technology transfer metrics have policy origins, and both have policy relevance. That fact is emphasized in this chapter, and it will be discussed in more detail in Chap. 8.

Chapter 3 provides the institutional context for the remainder of this book. The legislative and organizational history of the NHLBI is presented, as is the legislative history of the Small Business Innovation Research (SBIR) program and the Small Business Technology Transfer (STTR) program. These are the programs that funded the research

Table 1.1 Examples of Heart Disease Research Funded by the NHLBI

Formulation and Pharmacokinetics of Subcutaneous Administration of Deferiprone for Prevention of Chronic Heart Failure Following Hemorrhagic Myocardial Infarction

Approximately 50% of myocardial infarction (MI) patients progress to chronic heart failure (CHF) post-MI with a 5-year mortality rate of ~ 50% (rt300,000 US deaths annually). Recent studies have elucidated an obligate mechanism for progression to CHF and new therapeutic opportunities. The data indicate: (1) that hemorrhage is associated with larger MIs; (2) when normalized for infarct size, patients with hemorrhagic MIs (hMIs) are at greater risk for CHF; and (3) intramyocardial iron from hemorrhage persists for years and drives persistent macrophage recruitment, inflammation, fat deposition, and loss of heart function. Extensive data demonstrate that deferiprone (a generic iron chelator FDA approved for iron overload in thalassemia patients) renders iron functionally inert, suppresses fat deposition, reduces iron within hMI territories, and supports anatomical and functional recovery away from CHF in a large animal model of hMI. Yet, deferiprone has an exceptionally short half-life (1–2 hours). Even given 2- to 3-times daily, large gaps in blood levels (exposure) of deferiprone are evident, with implications for gaps in suppression of disease progression and iron removal. Also, deferiprone has low bioavailability due to ~ 70% first-pass metabolism in the liver to the inactive 3-O-glucuronide metabolite, which may be associated with at least some (possibly most?) side effects.

We propose that subcutaneous delivery of deferiprone using an infusion pump will provide continuous blood exposure to maintain iron in its inert state, will enable continuous iron removal, and will bypass first-pass metabolism and minimize exposure to deferiprone's primary metabolite. We further propose that a lower dose of deferiprone will prove highly efficacious. In Phase I SBIR studies, we will attain proof of concept that subcutaneous (SC) administration of deferiprone is efficient for the delivery of deferiprone while avoiding first-pass metabolism. In Phase II SBIR studies, we will evaluate administration using an infusion pump, we will determine the minimum dose for maximal efficacy, and we will attain initial safety data. Aim 1: We will prepare deferiprone from available API sources for subcutaneous delivery using established methods for optimal patient comfort and compliance. Purity of the API, oral, IV, and SC drug will be verified using published HPLC methods, and we will perform preliminary 1-month drug stability at ambient and accelerated storage conditions. Aim 2: We will establish LC/MS methods to quantify and identify deferiprone and its metabolites and perform pharmacokinetic analysis of SC administration as compared to IV and oral delivery. We anticipate rt90% bioavailability of SC deferiprone (compared to IV), no first-pass metabolism, and dose-linearity following SC administration. Impact: Foremost, this study holds the promise to be the first drug capable of removing an obligate driver of CHF in post-hMI patients. The product further holds the promise to reduce side-effects, maintain more patients on therapy, and ultimately enhance quality of life and life expectancy of hundreds of thousands of post-hMI patients each year.

(continued)

Table 1.1 (continued)

An In Vitro Electrophysiology System for High-Throughput Measurement of Cardiomyocyte Action Potential
Heart disease has been the #1 cause of fatality in the United States since 1950. Additionally, cardiovascular safety liability especially pro-arrhythmic risk remains a leading cause for the high attrition rate in drug development. For investigation of mechanisms and potential therapies for cardiac dysfunction, there has been strong demand from industry and academic alike for high quality, high-throughput assay of cardiac action potential (AP), a powerful biomarker for cardiac dysfunction. Unfortunately, existing techniques for measurement of AP, including electrical and optical methods, all suffer from severe limitations and are technically challenging and/or costly to execute at scale. These limitations are further compounded by the profound heterogeneity of human-derived cardiomyocytes. This Phase I proposal aims to develop a novel in vitro electrophysiology system that supports high-throughput measurement of intracellular AP (iAP) using human-derived cardiomyocytes. More specifically, we seek to demonstrate the feasibility for researcher even with limited expertise in electrophysiology to perform high-throughput iAP assay that includes data acquisition and analysis. Central to this electrophysiology system is a 3D nanoelectrode array (NEA) developed at Stanford University, which bridges the gap between intracellular and extracellular electrophysiology and enables high-quality and scalable recordings of iAP from many individual cardiomyocytes. Based on this NEA technology, Cyion Technologies has previously developed a first-generation electrophysiology system (Vincent) that records iAP signals from up to 60 discrete cardiomyocytes in a single-well NEA substrate. Built on this success, in this proposal we seek to develop an additional "plate-reader" option that measures 672 individual cardiomyocytes using a 96-well NEA substrate. We will also implement a software algorithm in user software for automated, batch analysis of iAP signals, which is necessary for higher-throughput assay.
Development of an RNA-based Anticoagulant and Antidote for Precise On/Off Coagulation Control During Cardiovascular Procedures
Each year, approximately one-third of all hospitalized patients in the US (corresponding to about 12 million Americans) receive unfractionated heparin (UFH) to prevent clotting during surgical and invasive medical procedures, such as open-heart surgery and transcatheter heart valve replacement, and to prevent postoperative clotting issues, such as deep vein thrombosis, and major ischemic events, such as pulmonary embolism, heart attack, and stroke. UFH is a fast-acting, reversible, and inexpensive anticoagulant drug that indirectly inhibits several clotting factors, including thrombin and Xa. However, UFH is associated with serious acute side effects, including hypersensitivity reactions. The non-linear dose response to UFH and a high degree of patient-to-patient and batch-to-batch variability lead to medication errors related to improper dosing, and these errors are among the most common and serious in clinical practice. An estimated 1–5% of patients who receive UFH experience an immune response known as heparin-induced thrombocytopenia (HIT), which is considered

(continued)

Table 1.1 (continued)

life threatening or results in death in 20–30% of affected patients. Additionally, up to 26% of cardiac surgery patients experience "heparin resistance," where achieving therapeutic anticoagulation requires excessive doses of UFH. As with any anticoagulant, treatment with UFH carries the risk of excessive bleeding, which can be fatal. UFH is reversed by protamine, which is also associated with serious side effects, including anaphylaxis and toxicity. Accurate determination of the dosing ratio of protamine to UFH is challenging, putting patients at risk for protamine overdose. In the context of medical procedures that require precise (i.e., immediate and titratable) hemostatic control, such as transcatheter heart valve replacement, these shortcomings are particularly challenging. Thus, there is a recognized, unmet medical need for new anticoagulant/reversal agent combinations that are safe and fast acting with a predictable dose response to enable more precise hemostatic control during medical procedures. Helixomer, Inc. is developing a novel polynucleotide-based anticoagulant/ antidote combination for intravenous anticoagulation. In vitro and in vivo data have demonstrated that Helixomer's anticoagulant drug, Hex01, and its antidote, Hex02, are highly specific and fast acting, with clear, predictable dose responses. Hex01 specifically binds to and directly inhibits thrombin, the enzyme responsible for fibrin deposition and clot formation. Hex02 base-pairs with and deactivates Hex01, reversing the anticoagulant effect by releasing thrombin. In this Direct-to-Phase II SBIR project, Helixomer will advance the preclinical development of Hex01 and Hex02 by (i) validating bioanalytical assays for Hex01 and Hex02 in plasma to support preclinical development, (ii) establishing scale-up manufacturing methods for Hex01, (iii) determining a dosing strategy for Hex01 and Hex02 in a porcine large-animal model, and (iv) defining safety and toxicity profiles for Hex01 and Hex02 and identifying the maximum tolerated dose through non-GLP dose range finding studies in rats and dogs. Successful completion of these critical preclinical studies will support subsequent pivotal GLP toxicology studies and IND submission.
Soft Robotic Sensor Arrays for Fast and Efficient Mapping of Cardiac Arrhythmias
Conform Medical is applying materials science, soft robotics, and stretchable electronics to revolutionize the mapping and ablation of the aberrant electrical signals underlying arrythmias, starting with ventricular tachycardia (VT), then expanding to other types of cardiac arrythmia such as atrial fibrillation (AFib). Cardiac electrophysiology specialists at hospitals and cardiac centers are commonly pained by the lack of tools to efficiently map ventricular foci with enough speed to diagnose VT. This wide, complex tachyarrhythmia is usually caused by ischemic heart disease, and VT, along with ventricular fibrillation (VF), are responsible for 75% of the 450,000 sudden cardiac deaths that occur yearly in the US Electrophysiological mapping is critical for VT management, especially for patients for whom VT cannot be well managed by pharmaceuticals alone. In these cases, treatment comprises a procedure in which VT is induced and a minimally invasive electrode catheter is used to map cardiac electrical signals and determine the source of the aberrant electrical pathways associated with the VT. Keeping these patients in a state of induced arrythmia is only safe for a short period of time, often just minutes. However, current mapping

(continued)

Table 1.1 (continued)

catheters are not able to acquire a sufficiently detailed activation map of the ventricle in such a short time. These limitations lead to suboptimal results, with nearly 90% of VT patients deemed 'unmappable'. Conform Medical addresses these critical needs with a novel device composed of soft robotic and stretchable electronic technology, which will enable fast and accurate cardiac mapping of ventricular foci. The device's soft robotic sensor array (SRSA) uniformly conforms 80 flexible sensors to the left ventricular tissue by hydraulically actuating an elastic thin-walled polymer in the form of a traditional basket mapping catheter. The soft robotic basket is integrated with a stretchable sensing array formed from low-cost, scalable flex-PCBs, and undergoes a proprietary laser-based processing method to render them highly stretchable. This innovative approach overcomes the main challenges in the development of a whole chamber basket catheter for cardiac mapping, namely scalable fabrication, integration, and conformability. The goal of this Phase I project is to de-risk the use of the technology in ventricles by optimizing delivery in 3D printed models that recapitulate the required catheter trackability and anatomic features/functions, validating its performance in vivo, and demonstrating compatibility with an open, commercial cardiac mapping system. The specific aims for this project are: (1) Optimize the catheter delivery system in a 3D printed heart model; (2) Demonstrate the functionality of the device in vivo in porcine models; and (3) Integrate the device with a commercial cardiac mapping system to determine accuracy of spatial mapping and validate the quality of electrical readings. This innovative technology will offer an answer the growing burden of ventricular arrhythmias, which calls for novel and effective therapies, and can also be applied to AFib, and other arrythmias.

Minimally Invasive High Intensity Therapeutic Ultrasound for the Treatment of Obstructive Hypertrophic Cardiomyopathy

Obstructive hypertrophic cardiomyopathy (oHCM) is a common inherited heart disease that can cause major limitations to daily acts of living, poor prognosis, and mortality. There are as many as 1.5 M people with HCM in the US alone, 2/3 of whom have the obstructive form of the disease with over 50k remaining refractory to medical management and are candidates for septal reduction therapy (SRT). Despite this, only ~ 1,200 patients per year of the 50k currently indicated receive SRT, leaving the vast majority of the most severe patients untreated. The reason for is the highly invasive nature of existing SRTs that cause frequency cardiac rhythm abnormalities requiring implantation of a pacemaker or cardioverter defibrillator (ICD) and have unacceptably high rates of peri- and post-procedural mortality (up to 10%). Additionally, many patients are unsuitable for existing SRT procedures due to existing co-morbidities and/or anatomical limitations. This Phase II SBIR proposes development of a novel treatment for oHCM by precisely targeting the source of the obstruction on the interventricular septum (IVS) using a novel high-intensity therapeutic ultrasound (HITU) catheter. Our approach takes a relatively safe, femoral venous approach to the right ventricle (RV) using existing delivery tools and knowhow within cardiac electrophysiology. Treatment focuses on delivery of HITU to selectively

(continued)

Table 1.1 (continued)

ablate the entire mid-myocardium of the IVS while sparing the cardiac conduction system on the sub-endocardium (His-Purkinje), thereby reducing risk of heart block requiring pacemaker or ICD insertion. This proposal builds upon the Phase I-equivalent work in acoustic physics, and pre-clinical proof of concept with a prototype catheter demonstrating that, by generating deep lesions in the mid-septum with an HITU, the IVS thickness can be reduced by approximately 30%. Based on catheter irrigation features and HITU's natural focusing characteristics sparing the sub-endocardium, heart block can be avoided even in the setting of extensive ablation in this region. The aims of this proposal will focus on maturation of catheter design elements and manufacturing methods to make the prototype device suitable for clinical evaluation, verify the functionality and safety of the system to relevant international safety standards (particularly IEC 60,601-2-62 standards), and validate the safety, efficacy, and durability of this therapy in acute and chronic (3-month) preclinical models via clinically accepted modalities (cardiac MRI, TTE, clinical pathology, gross pathology and histopathology). The information obtained in this grant will be used in direct support of early feasibility IDE submission with the FDA as part of a future phase of the grant. Commercialization of our system will bring lifesaving therapy to thousands of critically ill patients every year and eventually expand to treatment of HCM patients in earlier stages of the disease before long-standing obstructive hypertrophy resulted in irreversible health consequences.

The First Clinical Use of the BiVACOR Total Artificial Heart

Heart Failure (HF) is a devastating epidemic affecting more than 23 million patients worldwide; in the US alone, 1,000,000 new cases are reported each year. While heart transplantation provides the best treatment option for many patients, less than 6,000 procedures take place globally each year. Consequently, it is estimated that 50,000–100,000 patients could immediately benefit from mechanical circulatory support. Many circulatory support devices are available for patients who require left ventricular support, but few options exist for patients who would benefit from biventricular support. With the exception of transplantation, the optimal approach to biventricular failure is the replacement of the native heart with a Total Artificial Heart (TAH). Traditional approaches have used volume displacement pumps, which have inherent limitations due to their large size, flexing membranes, and valves that conspire to reduce the durability and lifetime of the device. The same limitations were observed throughout the early application of VAD technology, which prompted a transition to rotary blood pumps for size reduction and increased durability. Today, more than 60,000 patients are supported with rotary VADs. Capitalizing on the advantages of rotary blood pump technology, the BiVACOR TAH is small, reliable, blood-friendly and has inherently balanced blood flows. Under the previous SBIR grants, the system components of the BiVACOR TAH were significantly improved and validated on the benchtop and in vivo. BiVACOR has entered the final product development and manufacturing phase and wishes to utilize the SBIR II scheme to use the

(continued)

Table 1.1 (continued)

BiVACOR TAH system for the first time clinically via an FDA-approved Early Feasibility Study (EFS). To achieve this goal, the following specific aims will be completed: (1) clinical study initiation; (2) evaluate the safety and performance of the BIVACOR TAH in a clinical study; and (3) evaluate the outcomes of the Early Feasibility Study and identify required device updates. The commercial application and viability of this product will be demonstrated and will encourage additional investment for full commercialization. The world-wide impact of a commercially viable, long-term mechanical replacement to the failing human heart will be tremendous. The wait for patients desperately requiring a heart transplant will go from years to off-the-shelf availability, thereby quickly providing a vastly improved quality of life. Leveraging the successful durability and small size of similar technologies used for ventricular assistance into the BiVACOR rotary TAH provides a promising pathway to finally achieve the goal of a reliable, biocompatible, physiological, and ultimately practical replacement to the failing human heart.

Source https://www.sbir.gov/sbirsearch/award/all

projects considered in subsequent chapters. A descriptive emphasis is placed on the public sector resources allocated to these two programs, and illustrative examples of previously funded research projects are summarized in general terms in an effort to demonstrate the breadth of research funded through the NHLBI. While these research projects are not directly focused on heart disease, their emphasis is on lung and blood problems and diseases that indirectly affect the heart.

Several of the following chapters in this book rely on the NHLBI SBIR-funded project data. Chapter 4 provides information that includes knowledge transfer metrics from funded projects as well as characterizations of the firms that were funded to conduct that research. Background on the Congressional charge to the National Research Council (NRC) within the National Academies of Sciences, Engineering, and Medicine to establish such a database through surveys is presented.

Based on the survey data described in Chap. 4, knowledge transfer metrics are discussed in general terms and in specific terms in Chap. 5. The NHLBI SBIR data set contain information on 25 knowledge transfer metrics related to funded small firms, where the adjective *small* refers to firms with less than 500 employees. These metrics are discussed within the context of knowledge outflows, knowledge inflows, and two-way knowledge flows. The years of data coverage are 1992 through 2001.

Some readers might pause here to question our use of data that are over 25 years old. Such a reaction is perfectly reasonable. First, these are, to the best of our knowledge, the only public data available that focus on the NHLBI at a disaggregated level, meaning at the Institute level within the NIH. Second, the robustness of our findings might initiate additional Congressional inquiries into the funded research by the NHLBI through its SBIR program. Such a comparative study would allow policy makers to understand better trends in the social importance of NHLBI research.

Four specific knowledge transfer metrics are discussed in detail in Chap. 6. These metrics are commercialization from the NHLBI SBIR-funded research; and the number of patents, patent licenses, and scientific publications resulting from the funded research. The justification for an emphasis on these four knowledge outflow metrics is offered in terms of an emphasis on the extant economics and policy literatures and in terms of contemporary policy interests in these outflows. Descriptive information is presented on each of these metrics in an effort to inform the reader about multiple dimensions of the performance of funded projects. The characterizing dimensions considered are the ownership gender of the funded firms, the funded firms' research relationship with universities, and the funded firms' network relationship with other businesses (e.g., marketing and distribution agreements to enhance commercialization of the resulting new technology). This descriptive information is presented through bar charts and trend lines.

Chapter 7 addresses a counterfactual situation, namely the anticipated research behavior of a firm if it had not received the NHLBI SBIR funding. Our discussion of such a situation is relatively new to the economics and policy literatures; however, it might evoke a new policy discussion of research funding priorities for SBIR projects.

In the concluding Chap. 8, a number of key findings from the descriptive analysis from earlier chapters is summarized. Also included in Chap. 8 is a suggested roadmap for future research, be it Congressionally funded or not, that is needed to extend the preliminary findings that have been presented. More explicitly, this chapter provides a detailed roadmap for broad-based research directions that are suggested from the foundational analysis on public sector support of heart related and other NHLBI research. In addition, policy recommendations to further enhance the effectiveness of the NHLBI's funded heart disease and related research in small firms are offered. These US specific recommendations follow directly from the performance information presented in Chaps. 5 and 6; but the relevance of these recommendations may also be important for the international community that supports similar research to that of NHLBI.

CHAPTER 2

The Economic Importance of Knowledge Transfers

Abstract Knowledge transfer and technology transfer metrics are described in this chapter and are presented based on data reporting by the US Technology Partnerships Office at the National Institute of Standards and Technology. The relevant technology transfer metrics used in the United States for descriptive purposes are invention disclosures, patent applications filed, patents issued, Federal licenses, Federal income from licenses, Federal collaborative research and development (R&D) relationships, and science and engineering (S&E) articles published. A comparative reference is made to the knowledge transfer metrics commonly referred to by policy makers in the European Union.

In 2020, the Joint Research Centre of the European Commission's (EC's) science and knowledge service released a report entitled *Knowledge Transfer Metrics: Towards a European-Wide Set of Harmonised Indicators* (Campbell et al., 2020). The purpose of this EC report was "to provide evidence-based scientific support to the European policymaking process" (2020, p. 2). Motivating this report, which was built on earlier reports by Finne et al. (2009, 2011), is the economic and social importance of knowledge transfer (KT) as expressed in the following passage from the EC's report (2020, p. 6):

A. N. Link, A. C. O'Connor, *The Economics of Heart Disease Research*, Palgrave Advances in the Economics of Innovation and Technology, https://doi.org/10.1007/978-3-032-13547-6_2

> Knowledge Transfer (KT) aims to maximise the *two–way* [emphasis added] flow of technology, IP [intellectual property] and ideas. In turn this enables companies (existing and new) or other non-academic organisations and the public sector, to drive innovation leading to economic and social benefit and enables publicly funded research organisations (PROs) to advance research and teaching. KT is now a recognised activity in which PROs are expected to engage and [it] has been adopted as a part of the "third mission"[1] alongside teaching and research by many, but by no means all, PROs and universities across Europe. For many, KT is seen as an essential source of innovation and a mechanism for the dissemination of research results.

Having a common set of "harmonised indicators" is important for innovation policy in any country. Metrics, which often guide public sector resource allocations, influence the innovative behavior of organizations in both the private sector and the public sector (Choudhry and Ponzio, 2020; Hall, 2022). And, innovative behavior is fundamental to economic growth in both the short run and the long run.

The chapters in this book explore, in a descriptive manner, "the two–way flow of technology, IP and ideas" (Campbell et al., 2020, p. 6), quoted from the above passage from the EC's report, that are associated small firm research projects funded through the National Heart, Lung, and Blood Institute's (NHLBI's) Small Business Innovation Research (SBIR) program. Being descriptive in its character rather than analytical in a causal way, the intent of this book is to inform policy makers and academic scholars about policy-related activities within the NHLBI in an effort to not only draw attention to this Institute's extramural heart-related research programs but also to encourage a greater and more in-depth study of the NHLBI as an Institute. In other words, this book is intended only to describe *what has happened* within the NHLBI rather than offering hypotheses or empirical evidence about *what should have happened* within the NHLBI from an economic or policy perspective.

Given the social importance of NHLBI-related research, and the fact that the NHLBI has, to the best of our knowledge, yet to be studied from

[1] According to Compagnucci and Spigarelli (2020, p. 120,284) "[I]n recent years, there has been increasing pressure on Universities, to shift from mainly teaching and performing research, and adding a TM [Third Mission], portrayed as 'a contribution to society' ..." See their paper for a review of the academic literature related to TM research.

an economic perspective, the focus of this book seems appropriate. In fact, of the 21 Institutes within the National Institutes of Health (NIH), the only other Institute that has been studied from an in-depth economic perspective is the National Cancer Institute (NCI) (Link 2024b).

An excellent review of the limited, yet important, literature related to knowledge transfers is included in the Joint Research Centre of the European Commission's (EC's) report *Knowledge Transfer Metrics: Towards a European–Wide Set of Harmonised Indicators* (Campbell et al., 2020). However, what is most important for this book is to highlight what the Joint Research Centre considered to be the more fundamental knowledge transfer metrics. Those metrics are, in the order presented in the EC's report (and possibly in the order of importance to the EC) (Campbell et al., 2020, p. 16):

- Publication and presentations,
- Teaching,
- Networking/Events,
- Consultancy,
- Professional Development,
- Collaborative Research,
- Contract Research,
- Licensing, and
- Company Creation.

As described in the EC's report, these nine metrics or mechanism areas mirror the channels through which knowledge is perceived to be transferred in a two-way manner from and to an economic unit (e.g., a firm or organization) whether that economic unit resides in the private sector or in the public sector.

From these metrics, which were posited from a European perspective, there is a subset of technology transfer metrics that is commonly considered in the United States for policy purposes. Such a limited overlap is not a criticism of either the broad-based approach of the EC or the more limited and focused approach of most US technology transfer offices (federal technology transfer offices as well as university technology transfer offices).

The Technology Partnerships Office (TPO)[2] within the National Institute of Standards and Technology (NIST)[3] considers, from a data reporting perspective, the following seven metrics listed in the order of NIST's presentation (and possibly in the order of importance to the TPO):

- Invention disclosures,
- Patent applications filed,
- Patents issued,
- Federal licenses,
- Federal income from licenses,
- Federal collaborative R&D [research and development] relationships, and
- Science and engineering articles.

See Table 2.1 for NIST's comments about each of the TPO's technology transfer metrics. The TPO does not use the term ***knowledge transfer***.

Although the EC's technology transfer metrics were posited and studied from a European perspective, and the US technology transfer metrics reflect both a historical policy practice as well as a contemporary policy emphasis, discussed in Chap. 8, it is perhaps interesting to point out one differing ranked metric. Publications are the *first* [emphasis added] listed EC knowledge transfer metric, and the EC's report discussed quantifiable publication activity. In the TPO's discussion of metrics in Table 2.1, it is noted that "most Federal research results are transferred through publication of S&E [science and engineering] activities," but "a uniform tracking system for S&E articles across all Federal agencies does not exist." Thus,

[2] "The Technology Partnerships Office (TPO) within NIST plays a key role in the support of cutting-edge research that will promote US innovation and industrial competitiveness ... TPO's Vision: [For there to be] Engaged partnerships that benefit US research, innovation, and industrial competitiveness ... TPO's Mission: To enable and guide research collaborations and invention development and licensing to advance today's discoveries in ways that stimulate innovation, foster industrial competitiveness, enhance economic security, and improve our quality of life." See https://www.nist.gov/tpo/about-tpo. See also Link (2021, 2023a) for a discussion of the economics of metrology.

[3] NIST is the nation's metrology laboratory. [NIST's mission is to be] the world's leader in creating critical measurement solutions and promoting equitable standards. Our efforts stimulate innovation, foster industrial competitiveness, and improve the quality of life." See https://www.nist.gov/about-nist.

Table 2.1 Technology Partnerships Office Technology Transfer Metrics

Metric	*Comments*
Invention disclosures, Patent applications filed, and Patents issued	"The protection of intellectual property (IP) can be vital to attracting additional investment and product development resources necessary for early-stage technologies to be brought to their full commercial potential. Federal laboratory achievements in the areas of invention disclosures and patents issued are often cited as metrics of the active management of intellectual assets and technical know-how by Federal agencies."
Federal licenses	"Licensing is an important technology transfer mechanism that creates incentives for industry to invest the resources necessary to develop and commercialize nascent, leading-edge technologies. Successful development and commercialization of Federal technologies benefits the public and contributes to overall competitiveness and domestic economic growth. Without the ability to grant licenses and accompanying incentives to the non-Federal sector, federally developed innovations might be doomed to an idle future rather than developed into commercial products or services."
Federal income from licenses	"Licensing income includes income received for earned royalties from partners, license issue fees, minimum annual royalties, paid-up license fees, and reimbursement for full-cost recovery of goods and services provided by the lab to the licensee, including patent costs."
Federal collaborative R&D relationships	"Collaborative R&D [research and development] relationships between Federal laboratories and non-Federal collaborators are widely viewed as an effective and economical means of transferring technology and knowledge through joint research. These relationships create a mutually advantageous leveraging of Federal agency and collaborator resources and technical capabilities. They also provide avenues for both the collaborator and the Federal laboratory to gain new competencies and develop new skills. One frequently used mechanism for establishing joint research relationships is the CRADA [Cooperative

(continued)

Table 2.1 (continued)

Metric	*Comments*
	Research and Development Agreement], a multifaceted mechanism that can be used to address several kinds of partnership needs. 'Traditional CRADAs refer to formal collaborative R&D agreements between a Federal laboratory and non-Federal partners. Other special CRADA arrangements are used by Federal agencies to address special purpose applications such as material transfer agreements or agreements that facilitate technical assistance activities."
Science and engineering (S&E) articles	"Although IP has traditionally been tracked in terms of patents, licenses, and collaborative efforts, most Federal research results are transferred through publication of S&E articles. Unfortunately, a uniform tracking system for S&E articles across all Federal agencies does not exist."

Source NIST (2022, pp. 5–12.)

S&E publications are listed last just above and in Table 2.1. Both from a European perspective and a US perspective, publications are the primary mechanism for the transfer of technology-related knowledge, but they seem to be measured more completely (or more readily) in European research organizations than in US research organizations.

In the following Chap. 3, we provide the institutional context for the remainder of this book. The legislative and organizational history of NHLBI is presented as is the legislative history of the SBIR program. Briefly discussed are the Small Business Innovation Research (SBIR) program and the Small Business Technology Transfer (STTR) program from the perspective of its origin in an effort to provide context for the National Research Council (NRC) data used in the chapters that follow.

References

Campbell, A., C. Cavalade, C. Haunold, P. Karanikic, and A. Piccaluga. 2020. *Knowledge transfer metrics: towards a European-wide set of harmonised indicators*. Luxembourg: Publications Office of the European Union.

Compagnucci, L., and F. Spigarelli. 2020. The third mission of the university: a systematic literature review on potentials and constraints. *Technological Forecasting and Social Change* 161:120284.

Link, A. N. 2021. *The economics and science of measurement: a study of metrology.* Oxfordshire, UK: Routledge.

Link, A. N. 2023a. The economics of metrology: an exploratory study of the impact of measurement science on US productivity. *Economics of Innovation and New Technology* 32:213–222.

Link, A. N. 2024b. The globalization of the US Small Business Innovation Research (SBIR) program. *Annals of Science and Technology Policy* 8:3–243.

National Institute of Standards and Technology (NIST). 2022. *Federal laboratory technology transfer fiscal year 2020: Summary report to the President and Congress.* Gaithersburg, MD: National Institute of Standards and Technology.

CHAPTER 3

The NHLBI and Its Small Business Research Programs

Abstract This chapter provides historical institutional and legislative information about the formation of the National Heart, Lung, and Blood Institute (NHLBI), and it describes the mission of the NHLBI along with the mission of the other Institutes within the National Institutes of Health (NIH). The Small Business Innovation Research (SBIR) program is also discussed in terms of its legislative history and its specific mission and goals within the NIH and the NHLBI. Numerous graphs are included to illustrate the budget history of NIH and the NHLBI and the research award history of the SBIR program within the NIH and the NHLBI. The appendix to the chapter provides abstract summaries of representative research projects funded through the SBIR program.

3.1 The NHLBI

The organizational foundation for what would become the National Institutes of Health), (NIH) traces to July 16, 1798, when President John Adams signed into law the Act for the Relief of Sick and Disabled Seamen of 1798.[1] The Act of 1798 authorized twenty cents to be deducted from each seaman's wages each month to fund the care for

[1] The following abbreviated history draws directly from Link and O'Connor (2025). There are only so many ways to chronicle historical events; thus, duplication of text is inevitable.

A. N. Link, A. C. O'Connor, *The Economics of Heart Disease Research*, Palgrave Advances in the Economics of Innovation and Technology,
https://doi.org/10.1007/978-3-032-13547-6_3

those sick and disabled. The establishment of the Marine Hospital Service grew from this legislation.[2] The first Marine Hospital, founded in 1804, was located in Boston, Massachusetts.

In 1870, President Ulysses S. Grant reorganized the Marine Hospital Service to be a national hospital system with a centralized administration under the leadership of a medical officer who was to be known as the Supervising Surgeon (and later that title would become simply Surgeon General). In April 1878, President Rutherford B. Hayes signed the National Quarantine Act of 1878 assigning to the Marine Hospital Service the responsibility to control diseases coming into the United Sates.[3] Then, in April 1879, President Hayes appointed Dr. and Commodore John Hamilton as the Supervising Surgeon General (a new title). In response to the on-going yellow fever epidemic—the so-called Epidemic of 1878—Surgeon General Hamilton selected Dr. Joseph J. Kinyoun to establish a federal laboratory of medical bacteriology, which later would be known as the Hygienic Laboratory. This laboratory was initially located at the Stapleton Hospital on Staten Island, a borough of New York city. In June 1891, President Benjamin Harrison appointed Dr. and Commodore Walter Wyman as the nation's third Surgeon General (the new shortened title),[4] and in that same year Wyman moved the federal laboratory of medical bacteriology—the Hygienic Laboratory—to Washington, DC, and it became known formally as the Hygienic Laboratory in the Marine Hospital Service.

On May 23, 1930, with the passage of An Act to Establish and Operate a National Institute [singular] of Health of 1930 (Public Law 71–251), also known as the Ransdell Act of 1930,[5] the name of the Hygienic Laboratory was changed to the National Institute [singular] of Health (NIH). With the subsequent establishment of additional research units, the first being the National Cancer Institute (NCI) in 1937, the organization's name was changed again in 1948 to the National Institutes [plural]

A more detailed discussion of the NIH and the National Heart, Lung, and Blood Institute (NHLBI) is also in Link and O'Connor (2025).

[2] See https://www.marinehospital.org/publichealth.htm.

[3] See https://www.pbs.org/wgbh/americanexperience/features/fever-1878-epidemic/.

[4] See https://en.wikipedia.org/wiki/Surgeon_General_of_the_United_States.

[5] The Act was sponsored by Senator Joseph E. Ransdell of Louisiana. See https://history.nih.gov/display/history/WWI+and+the+Ransdell+Act+of+1930.

of Health (NIH). The move from Washington, DC to the NIH's present location in Bethesda, Maryland, began in 1938.

In 1948, the National Heart Institute (NHI) was established within the NIH; it is the second oldest Institute behind the NCI.[6] In 1969, the scope of the NHI's research expanded, and the Institute was renamed the National Heart and Lung Institute (NHLI). And in 1976, the NHLI became the National Heart, Lung, and Blood Institute (NHLBI) reflecting the expansion of blood-related research in the Institute. The NHLBI is currently the fourth largest Institute within the NIH in terms of public sector financial support.

Table 3.1 summarizes several milestone events in the legislative history of the NHLBI.

Table 3.2 lists the 21 Institutes currently within the NIH. In addition to these Institutes, there are also 6 Centers; the roles of these Centers are discussed in detail in Link and O'Connor (2025).[7]

The NHLBI is the focal NIH Institute for this book for several reasons, as previously stated, but perhaps the most important reason, aside from the conspicuous absence of other NHLBI-focused studies, is that heart disease is the leading cause of death in the United States, as emphasized in Chap. 1, and that fact alone perhaps warrants an additional emphasis on research funded through the NHLBI.[8] In addition, to the best of our knowledge, this book represents the first systematic effort to describe

Table 3.1 Milestone Events in the Legislative History of the NHLBI

June 16, 1948: President Harry S. Truman signed the National Heart Act, creating and establishing the National Heart Institute (NHI) in the Public Health Service (PHS) and the National Advisory Heart Council
November 10, 1969: The NHI was renamed the National Heart and Lung Institute (NHLI), reflecting expansion of functions
June 25, 1976: The NHLI was renamed the National Heart, Lung, and Blood Institute (NHLBI), reflecting an expansion in blood-related activities within the Institute

Source https://www.nih.gov/about-nih/what-we-do/nih-almanac/national-heart-lung-blood-institute-nhlbi
Note An earlier version of this table was in Link and O'Connor (2025)

[6] See Link (2024).

[7] See https://www.nih.gov/institutes-nih/list-institutes-centers.

[8] See https://injuryfacts.nsc.org/all-injuries/deaths-by-demographics/all-leading-causes-of-death/.

Table 3.2 Institutes within the NIH, by Year Established

Institute Name (Institute Acronym)	*Year Established*	*Description*
National Cancer Institute (NCI)	1937	"NCI conducts and supports research that will lead to a future in which we can prevent cancer before it starts, identify cancers that do develop at the earliest stage, eliminate cancers through innovative treatment interventions, and biologically control those cancers that we cannot eliminate so they become manageable, chronic diseases."
National Heart, Lung, and Blood Institute (NHLBI)	1948	"NHLBI stimulates basic discoveries about the causes of disease, enables the translation of basic discoveries into clinical practice, fosters training and mentoring of emerging scientists and physicians, and communicates research advances to the public."
National Institute of Allergy and Infectious Diseases (NIAID)	1948	"NIAID research strives to understand, treat, and ultimately prevent the myriad infectious, immunologic, and allergic diseases that threaten millions of human lives."
National Institute of Dental and Craniofacial Research (NIDCR)	1948	"NIDCR provides leadership for a national research program designed to understand, treat, and ultimately prevent the infectious and inherited craniofacial-oral-dental diseases and disorders that compromise millions of human lives."
National Institute of Mental Health (NIMH)	1949	"NIMH provides national leadership dedicated to understanding, treating, and preventing mental illnesses through basic research on the brain and behavior, and through clinical, epidemiological, and services research."

(continued)

Table 3.2 (continued)

Institute Name (Institute Acronym)	*Year Established*	*Description*
National Institute of Diabetes and Digestive and Kidney Diseases (NIDDK)	1950	"The mission of the NIDDK is to conduct and support medical research and research training and to disseminate science-based information on diabetes and other endocrine and metabolic diseases; digestive diseases, nutritional disorders, and obesity; and kidney, urologic, and hematologic diseases, to improve people's health and quality of life."
National Institute of Neurological Disorders and Stroke (NINDS)	1950	"The mission of NINDS is to seek fundamental knowledge about the brain and nervous system and to use that knowledge to reduce the burden of neurological disease. To accomplish this goal the NINDS supports and conducts basic, translational, and clinical research on the normal and diseased nervous system."
National Library of Medicine (NLM)	1956	"NLM collects, organizes, and makes available biomedical science information to scientists, health professionals, and the public … NLM conducts and supports research in biomedical communications; creates information resources for molecular biology, biotechnology, toxicology, and environmental health; and provides grant and contract support for training, medical library resources, and biomedical informatics and communications research."
Eunice Kennedy Shriver National Institute of Child Health and Human Development (NICHD)	1962	"NICHD leads research and training to understand human development, improve reproductive health, enhance the lives of children and

(continued)

Table 3.2 (continued)

Institute Name (Institute Acronym)	*Year Established*	*Description*
		adolescents, and optimize abilities for all."
National Institute of General Medical Sciences (NIGMS)	1962	"NIGMS supports basic research that increases understanding of biological processes and lays the foundation for advances in disease diagnosis, treatment and prevention. NIGMS-funded scientists investigate how living systems work at a range of levels, from molecules and cells to tissues, whole organisms and populations."
National Eye Institute (NEI)	1968	"[NEI's] mission is to conduct and support research, training, health information dissemination, and other programs with respect to blinding eye diseases, visual disorders, mechanisms of visual function, preservation of sight, and the special health problems and requirements of the blind."
National Institute of Environmental Health Sciences (NIEHS)	1969	"The mission of the NIEHS is to discover how the environment affects people in order to promote healthier lives."
National Institute on Alcohol Abuse and Alcoholism (NIAAA)	1970	"NIAAA conducts research focused on improving the treatment and prevention of alcoholism and alcohol-related problems to reduce the enormous health, social, and economic consequences of this disease."
National Institute on Aging (NIA)	1974	"NIA leads a national program of research on the biomedical, social, and behavioral aspects of the aging process; the prevention of age-related diseases and disabilities; and the promotion of a better quality of life for all older Americans."

(continued)

Table 3.2 (continued)

Institute Name (Institute Acronym)	*Year Established*	*Description*
National Institute on Drug Abuse (NIDA)	1974	"The mission of the NIDA is to advance science on the causes and consequences of drug use and addiction and to apply that knowledge to improve individual and public health."
National Institute of Arthritis and Musculoskeletal and Skin Diseases (NIAMS)	1986	"NIAMS supports research into the causes, treatment, and prevention of arthritis and musculoskeletal and skin diseases, the training of basic and clinical scientists to carry out this research, and the dissemination of information on research progress in these diseases."
National Institute of Nursing Research (NINR)	1986	"The mission of the NINR is to lead nursing research to solve pressing health challenges and inform practice and policy—optimizing health and advancing health equity into the future."
National Institute on Deafness and Other Communication Disorders (NIDCD)	1988	"NIDCD conducts and supports biomedical research and research training on normal mechanisms as well as diseases and disorders of hearing, balance, smell, taste, voice, speech, and language that affect 46 million Americans."
National Human Genome Research Institute (NHGRI)	1989	"NHGRI's work now encompasses a broad range of research aimed at expanding understanding of human biology and improving human health. In addition, a critical part of NHGRI's mission continues to be the study of the ethical, legal and social implications of genome research."
National Institute of Biomedical Imaging and Bioengineering (NIBIB)	2000	"The mission of the NIBIB is to transform through engineering the understanding of disease and its

(continued)

Table 3.2 (continued)

Institute Name (Institute Acronym)	*Year Established*	*Description*
		prevention, detection, diagnosis, and treatment."
National Institute on Minority Health and Health Disparities (NIMHD)	2010	"NIMHD plans, reviews, coordinates, and evaluates all minority health and health disparities research and activities of the National Institutes of Health; conducts and supports research in minority health and health disparities; promotes and supports the training of a diverse research workforce; translates and disseminates research information; and fosters innovative collaborations and partnerships."

Source https://www.nih.gov/institutes-nih/list-institutes-centers
Note An earlier version of this table was in Link and O'Connor (2025)

NHLBI-funded SBIR projects. As such, given the social importance of the research of NHLBI, our descriptive picture of dimensions of research performance might motivate additional academic and policy emphasis on this particular Institute. In addition, the overall picture that we paint through our descriptive summaries in the following chapters might inform the Congress about dimensions of research performance that should be investigated in future studies of the NIH's other Institutes, in general, and about the role of the Small Business Innovation Research (SBIR) program in support of those Institutes, in particular.

The current mission of the NHLBI is (NHLBI, undated, p. 4):

> The National Heart, Lung, and Blood Institute (NHLBI) provides global leadership for a research, training, and education program to promote the prevention and treatment of heart, lung, and blood diseases and enhance the health of all individuals so that they can live longer and more fulfilling lives …

The NHLBI has four strategic goals and eight strategic objectives. The four strategic goals are: Understand human biology, Reduce human disease, Develop a workforce and resources, and Advance translational research. These four strategic goals are enumerated in Table 3.3.

Table 3.3 Strategic Goals of the NHLBI

Strategic Goal	*Description*
Understand human biology	"To expand knowledge of the molecular, cellular, and physiological mechanisms governing the normal function of HLBS [Heart, Lung, Blood, and Sleep Health] systems as essential elements for sustaining human health."
Reduce human disease	"To extend our knowledge of the pathobiology of HLBS disorders and enable clinical investigations that advance the prediction, prevention, preemption, treatment, and cures of human diseases."
Develop workforce and resources	"To enable and develop a diverse biomedical workforce equipped with the essential research resources to pursue emerging opportunities in science."
Advance translational research	"To facilitate innovation and accelerate research translation across the entire research spectrum, bridging basic to clinical, clinical to practice, and population to health impact."

Source https://www.nhlbi.nih.gov/about/strategic-vision/goals-and-objectives

The eight strategic objectives of the NHLBI are: Understand normal biological function and resilience; Investigate newly discovered pathobiological mechanisms important to the onset and progression of Heart, Lung, Blood, and Sleep Health (HLBS) diseases; Investigate factors that account for differences in health among populations; Identify factors that account for individual differences in pathobiology and in responses to treatments; Develop and optimize novel diagnostic and therapeutic strategies to prevent, treat, and cure HLBS diseases; Optimize clinical and implementation research to improve health and reduce disease; Leverage emerging opportunities in data science to open new frontiers in HLBS research; and Further develop, diversify, and sustain a scientific workforce capable of accomplishing the NHLBI's mission. These eight objectives are enumerated in Table 3.4.

For purposes of comparison, Fig. 3.1 shows constant dollar federal allocations to the NIH, and Fig. 3.2 shows constant dollar federal allocations to the NHLBI by fiscal year (FY). The constant dollar values in these figures are inflation-adjusted by the Gross Domestic Product (GDP), and they are in 2022 dollars ($2022). The periods of increase in federal allocations stopped in FY 2003; both budgets peaked in that fiscal year. Both budgets decreased thereafter, perhaps exacerbated by the Great

Table 3.4 Strategic Objectives of the NHLBI

Strategic Objective	*Description*
Understand normal biological function and resilience	"Understanding normal biology is the backbone of all biomedical science. It is essential for understanding homeostatic maintenance, predicting how biological systems respond to their environment, and recognizing disease and targets for intervention. Research on normal biological function ... can help us to better define health and understand the earliest origin of disease processes."
Investigate newly discovered pathobiological mechanisms important to the onset and progression of HLBS diseases	"Discovering new pathobiological mechanisms and understanding them is critical for improving heart, lung, blood, and sleep (HLBS) health. Such discoveries and research can potentially lead to clinical and implementation studies, which in turn can inform new therapeutic strategies and clinical practice. Important areas to focus on, with the help of emerging technologies such as molecular imaging and nanotechnology, include mechanisms involved in the pathogenesis of rare and common diseases, disease-related structural and functional changes, and the clinical significance of these changes."
Investigate factors that account for differences in health among populations	"Variations exist between populations ... in susceptibility and resilience to heart, lung, blood, and sleep (HLBS) diseases and in disease course and outcomes. While some of these variations are caused by genetic and other biological factors, a wide range of behavioral factors and socioeconomic inequities also contribute to health disparities. Research is needed to better understand the causes of population health differences and to identify strategies to effectively address these differences."
Identify factors that account for individual differences in pathobiology and in responses to treatments	"Research advances in areas such as genomics and other 'omics' (e.g., proteomics, metabolomics) have provided new opportunities to deepen our

(continued)

Table 3.4 (continued)

Strategic Objective	*Description*
	understanding of heart, lung, blood, and sleep (HLBS) pathobiological processes and how these vary among individual patients. Accelerating progress toward precise, individualized prevention efforts and medical interventions will require research into biological factors, environmental exposures, and other influences that account for differences in pathobiology and unique responses to treatment (including drug reactions and other adverse events)."
Develop and optimize novel diagnostic and therapeutic strategies to prevent, treat, and cure HLBS diseases	"Recent scientific and technological developments offer especially promising opportunities to prevent disease, manage and treat illness, and promote resilience. These wide-ranging developments include, but are not limited to, new gene editing techniques that could safely treat and prevent heart, lung, blood, and sleep (HLBS) diseases, 'smart' tools that could monitor and adjust biological processes, techniques that modulate stem cell or immune system signaling to reduce disease risk, and advances in materials science that could yield vastly improved implant devices."
Optimize clinical and implementation research to improve health and reduce disease	"New methodologies, research frameworks, and resources need to be developed to refine the conduct of clinical studies and implementation research, while also improving the overall efficiency and effectiveness of the research enterprise. Current challenges include difficulties in recruitment of research participants and effective translation of knowledge gained from these studies into programs and policies that improve health at the clinic and community levels."

(continued)

Table 3.4 (continued)

Strategic Objective	*Description*
Leverage emerging opportunities in data science to open new frontiers in HLBS research	"New technologies, from 'omics' platforms to high-throughput screening, have generated vast amounts of data that have the potential to provide new insights into the preemption and precise treatment of heart, lung, blood, and sleep (HLBS) disorders. Unfortunately, only a small portion of this data is being optimally assessed and incorporated into practice. Developing innovative approaches to the integration, analysis, and interpretation of data from multiple sources will be essential."
Further develop, diversify, and sustain a scientific workforce capable of accomplishing the NHLBI's mission	"Needed new approaches will ensure the continuing development of a diverse scientific workforce equipped with the relevant skills, knowledge, and resources to tackle future heart, lung, blood, and sleep (HLBS) challenges. This goal will require strategic interventions all along the research career continuum, including K to 12 education, collegiate and postdoctoral studies, and career development from early investigator to senior scientist. While this is relevant in all areas of development, particular attention is warranted for under-represented groups in science. Collaborative partnerships will be critical to collectively work toward the challenge of expanding the exposure of young students to the wonders of science and sustain that interest through college and graduate education. It is also critical to embrace research training as a lifelong exploration of scientific curiosity in which the NIH promotes the adoption of new disciplines, tools, and technologies as the scientific and public health landscape continually undergoes dynamic change."

Source https://www.nhlbi.nih.gov/about/strategic-vision

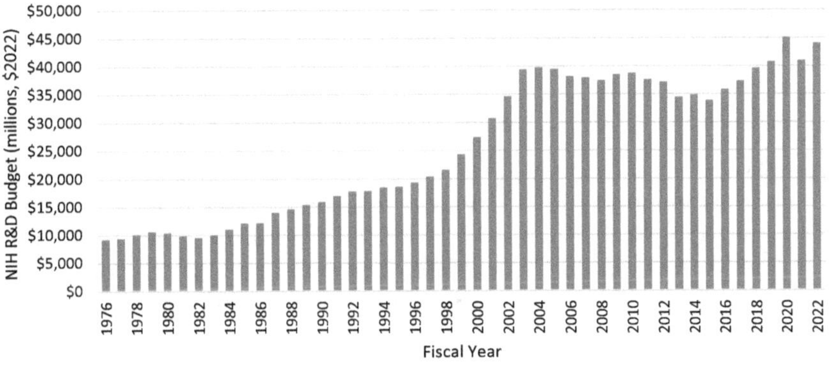

Fig. 3.1 R&D Budget of the NIH, by Fiscal Year 1976–2022 (millions, $2022). *Source* https://www.aaas.org/programs/r–d-budget-and-policy/historical-trends-federal-rd. *Note* The government's fiscal year changed from July 1—June 30 to October 1—September 30 in 1976

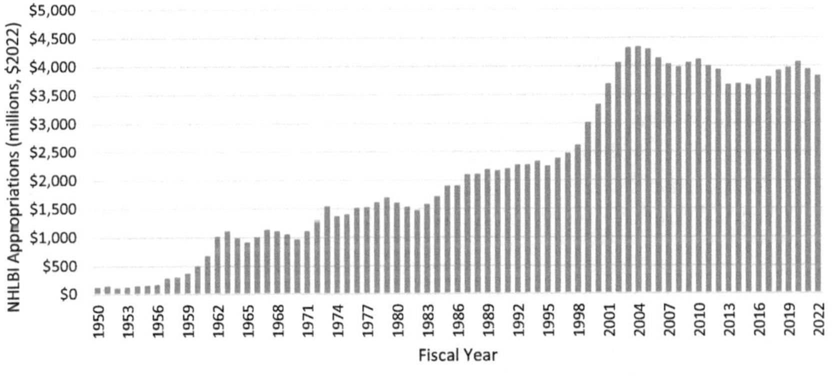

Fig. 3.2 Appropriations to the NHLBI, by Fiscal Year 1950–2022 (millions, $2022). *Source* https://www.nih.gov/about-nih/what-we–do/nih-almanac/appropriations-section-1. *Note* The government's fiscal year changed from July 1—June 30 to October 1—September 30 in 1976

Recession beginning in late FY 2007.[9] The NIH budget, but not the NHLBI budget, appears to be on the increase beginning in FY 2020.

3.2 The SBIR and STTR Programs[10]

The passage of the Small Business Act of 1953 (Public Law 163) was a milestone event in the US history of support for small firms. Soon thereafter, the Small Business Act of 1958 withdrew Title II of Public Law 163, and the Congress legislated a separate act also called the Small Business Act of 1958. After a series of amendments to the Act of 1958, the extant legislation was amended yet again through the Small Business Innovation Development Act of 1982 (Public Law 97–219).[11]

The Act of 1982 describes the general economic purpose of the Small Business Innovation Research (SBIR) program through its prefacing statement about the economic importance of innovation for the US economy, and through statements in the Act about the role of small firms in the innovation process.

The purpose statement for the Act of 1982, and thus for the SBIR program, is as follows:

The purposes of the Act are—

1. to stimulate technological innovation;
2. to use small business to meet Federal research and development [R&D] needs;
3. to foster and encourage participation by minority and disadvantaged persons in technological innovation; and
4. to increase private sector commercialization of innovations derived from Federal research and development.

[9] The National Bureau of Economic Research (NBER) dates the Great Recession from December 2007 to June 2009. See https://www.nber.org/research/data/us-business-cycle-expansions-and-contractions.

[10] We have written about the SBIR and STTR program on numerous occasions so duplication of some text is inevitable.

[11] A more detailed discussion of the Small Business Act of 1953 and the SBIR program in general is in Link (2024) and in the references therein. A complete discussion of the program's eligibility requirements is at: https://www.sbir.gov/tutorials/program-basics/tutorial-2.

The SBIR program was further defined in the Act of 1982 through the description of the phases of research that can be funded by the program. As stated in the Act of 1982, there is:

> … a first phase, [a Phase I], for determining, insofar as possible, the scientific and technical merit and feasibility of ideas submitted pursuant to SBIR program solicitations [and] a second phase, [a Phase II], to further develop the proposed ideas [in Phase I] to meet the particular program needs.

According to Gallo's most recent Congressional Research Service (CRS) report on the SBIR and Small Business Technology Transfer (STTR) programs (2022, p. 5), an agency may currently issue a Phase II award in an amount up to $1,838,436, although an agency may seek a waiver from the Small Business Administration (SBA) to exceed that amount. At the National Institutes of Health (NIH), there are other Small Business Program phases besides the SBIR and STTR Phase I and Phase II grants, as described in Table 3.5.[12]

To fund the above purposes, the Act of 1982 explicitly states that the SBIR program is to be a set-aside program.[13] Currently, through the SBIR and STTR Extension Act of 2022 (Public Law 117–183), the set aside amount to fund an agency's SBIR program is 3.2% of its extramural research budget.[14] At the NIH, the SBIR program and the STTR program are collectively the NIH's Small Business Programs, and they are also known as being a portion of America's Seed Fund.[15]

The SBIR and STTR programs fall under the umbrella of NIH's SEED (Small Business Education and Entrepreneurial Development) office, although each individual institute with more than $100 million in extramural

[12] As will be discussed in Chap. 4, the data used in this book relate to Phase II NHLBI SBIR research projects.

[13] As stated in the Act of 1982: "Each Federal agency which has an extramural budget for research or research and development in excess of $100,000,000 for fiscal year 1982, or any fiscal year thereafter, shall expend not less than 0.2 per centum of its extramural budget in fiscal year 1983 or in such subsequent fiscal year as the agency has such budget …"

[14] For a discussion of the STTR program see Link (2023).

[15] See https://seed.nih.gov/small-business-funding/small-business-program-basics/understanding-sbir-sttr.

Table 3.5 NIH Small Business Program Funding Phases

Phases	*Description*
Phase I	"A Phase I award helps you focus on the feasibility, technical merit, and commercial potential of your research project."
Phase II	"A Phase II award lets you continue the research and development efforts initiated in Phase I. Once you've reached your Phase I milestones, you can apply for a Phase II award, even before the end of the Phase I award. You may submit your application for a Phase II award up to six receipt dates after your Phase I budget period expires."
Fast-Track	"The Fast-Track process allows you to submit both Phase I and Phase II in one application for review. The Fast-Track mechanism can minimize the funding gap between phases but requires a fully developed Phase II application/plan at the time of submission."
Direct to Phase II (SBIR only)	"If your project has already demonstrated feasibility, but you have not received a Phase I SBIR or STTR, you can apply for a Direct to Phase II award and bypass Phase I."
Phase IIB	"Some NIH Institutes and Centers offer Phase IIB awards for Phase II projects that require extraordinary time and effort beyond the standard Phase II period of [two] years."
Commercialization Readiness Pilot (CRP) Program	"The Commercialization Readiness Pilot (CRP) Program provides awarded Phase II and Phase IIB small businesses technical assistance and funding for late-stage development."

Source https://seed.nih.gov/small-business-funding/small-business-program-basics/understanding-sbir-sttr

research funding operates its own dedicated small business office. The mission of the SEED office is:[16]

> ... to accelerate the conversion of scientific discoveries into healthcare solutions. SEED envisions a world where scientists are empowered to improve the lives of patients and their families.

[16] See https://seed.nih.gov/aboutseed.

This mission is in concert with the NIH's four core business objectives:[17]

> Identify and scale approaches that enable investigators to convert scientific discoveries into impactful healthcare solutions; Coordinate early-stage product development activities across the NIH; Inspire and support a diverse entrepreneurial workforce; [and] Demonstrate NIH's role in improving patient care and driving economic growth.

Two of the small business funding mechanisms to accomplish these objectives are the SBIR and STTR programs. The SBIR program is emphasized in the remaining chapters of this book because the data available for the analysis that follows in this book are only for SBIR (rather than SBIR and STTR) funded projects.

Ten agencies, in addition to the NIH within the Department of Health and Human Services (HHS), participate in the SBIR program. These agencies and organizations are (alphabetically): the Departments of Agriculture (USDA), Commerce (DOC), Defense (DOD), Education (ED), Energy (DOE), Homeland Security (DHS), Transportation (DOT), and the Environmental Protection Agency (EPA), the National Aeronautics and Space Administration (NASA), and the National Science Foundation (NSF).

3.3 The NHLBI SBIR Program

The mission and goals of the broader NIH SBIR program are similar to the mission and goals of the SBIR program in general. The NIH SBIR mission and goals are:[18]

- Stimulate technological innovation;
- Meet federal research and development needs;
- Increase private sector commercialization of innovations developed through federal R&D funding; and

[17] See https://seed.nih.gov/aboutseed.

[18] See https://seed.nih.gov/small-business-funding/small-business-program-basics/understanding-sbir-sttr.

- Foster and encourage participation in innovation and entrepreneurship by socially and economically disadvantaged (SDB) persons and women-owned small businesses (WOSB).[19]

As we pointed out above, the current legislated set aside amount to fund an agency's SBIR program is 3.2 % of its extramural research budget. Figure 3.3 shows, by fiscal year (FY), the Phase I award and obligated amounts (1000s) of support for NIH projects in current dollars. Figure 3.4 shows, by fiscal year, these amounts (1000s) in constant 2022 dollars ($2022). The trend in both metrics is positive as shown by the trend lines imposed on both of the figures, but the trend is visually more positive in Fig. 3.3 due to the inflationary component embedded in the current dollar amounts. The decline in both metrics after FY 2004 preceded the Great Recession.[20] The post-Covid-19 pandemic[21] trend, which began slightly ahead of the official start of the Covid-19 pandemic (March 2020), is somewhat more pronounced in constant dollars (Fig. 3.4) than in current dollars (Fig. 3.3). In neither case was the post-Covid-19 pandemic decline in funding as dramatic as was the pre-Great Recession decline in funding in 2007.

Figures 3.5 shows, by fiscal year, the Phase II award and obligated amounts (1000s) of support for NIH projects in current dollars. Figure 3.6 shows, by fiscal year, these amounts (1000s) in constant 2022 dollars ($2022). Again, the trend in both metrics is positive as shown by the trend lines imposed on both of the figures. The decline in both metrics in FY 2007 preceded the Great Recession, and the decline coincided with the

[19] "A socially and economically disadvantaged small business concern is one that is at least 51% owned and managed by one or more socially and economically disadvantaged people (who also control the day-to-day operations). In this context, control means making policy decisions. Operate means being actively involved in day-to-day management ... A member of any of the following groups: Black Americans, Hispanic Americans, Native Americans, Asian-Pacific Americans, Subcontinent Asian Americans, other groups designated from time to time by the Small Business Administration (SBA) to be socially disadvantaged, and any other individual found to be socially and economically disadvantaged by SBA pursuant to Section 8(a) of the Small Business Act, 15 U.S.C.; 637(a). See https://seedfund.nsf.gov/how-to-submit/definitions/.

[20] The National Bureau of Economic Research (NBER) dates the Great Recession from December 2007 to June 2009. See https://www.nber.org/research/data/us-business-cycle-expansions-and-contractions.

[21] The Center for Disease Control (CDC) dates the start of the Covid-19 pandemic as March 2020. See https://www.cdc.gov/museum/timeline/covid19.html.

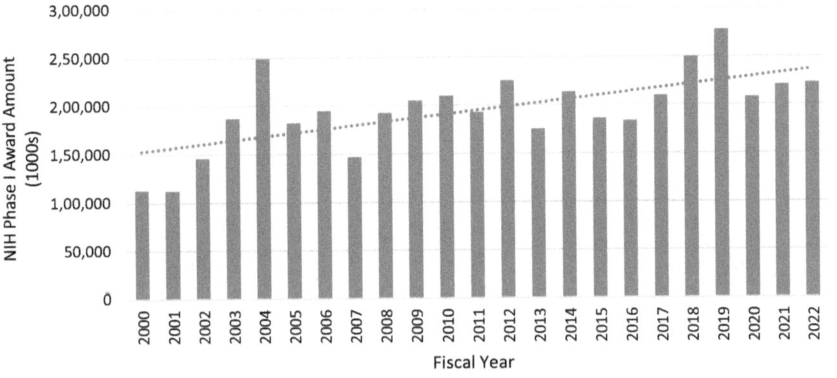

Fig. 3.3 Trend in NIH Phase I SBIR Awards and Obligated Amounts, by Fiscal Year (1000s, current dollars) 2000–2022. *Source* https://www.sbir.gov/sbir search/award/all. *Note* The trend line was generated through Excel

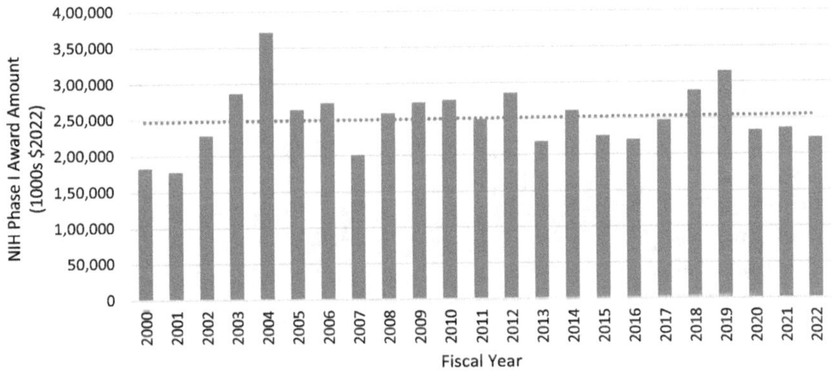

Fig. 3.4 Trend in NIH Phase I SBIR Awards and Obligated Amounts, by Fiscal Year (1000s, constant $2022) 2000–2022. *Source* https://www.sbir.gov/sbir search/award/all. *Note* The trend line was generated through Excel

decline in Phase I award and obligated amounts in both current and constant dollars. And, the post-Covid-19 pandemic decline in constant dollar funding (Fig. 3.6) was more dramatic than in current dollars (Fig. 3.5), which was not a decline at all.

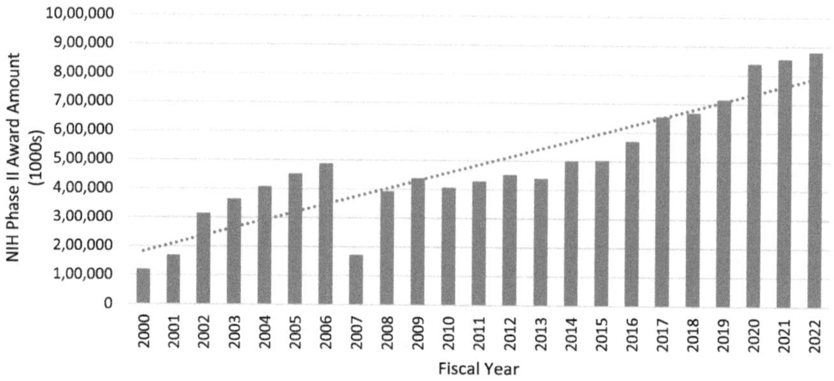

Fig. 3.5 Trend in NIH Phase II SBIR Awards and Obligated Amounts, by Fiscal Year (1000s, current dollars) 2000–2022. *Source* https://www.sbir.gov/sbir search/award/all. *Note* The trend line was generated through Excel

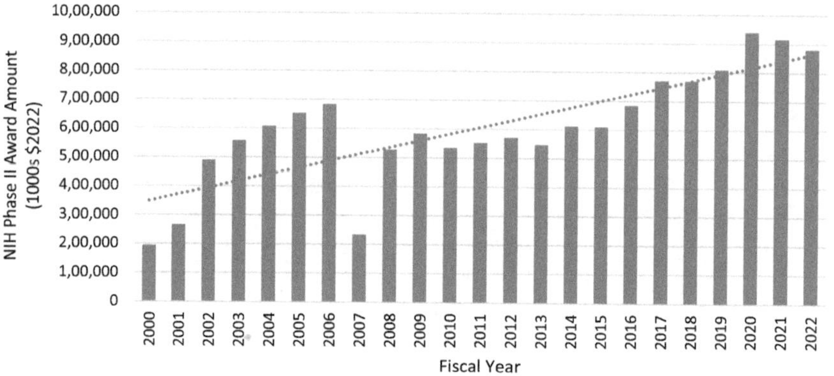

Fig. 3.6 Trend in NIH Phase II SBIR Awards, by Fiscal Year (1000s, constant $2022) 2000–2022. *Source* https://www.sbir.gov/sbirsearch/award/all. *Note* The trend line was generated through Excel

Specifically, regarding the mission and goals of the NHLBI SBIR program:[22]

[22] See https://www.sbir.gov/node/361231.

> The NHLBI SBIR program fosters basic, applied, and clinical research on all product and service development related to the mission of the NHLBI. The NHLBI plans, conducts, fosters, and supports an integrated and coordinated program of basic research, clinical investigation, and trials, observational studies, and demonstration and education projects. The Institute's mission includes studies related to the causes, prevention, diagnosis, and treatment of heart, blood vessel, lung, blood, sleep disorders, and blood resources management. Studies are conducted in its own laboratories and by other scientific institutions and individuals supported by research grants and contracts. The NHLBI SBIR program fosters basic, applied, and clinical research on all product and service development related to the mission of the NHLBI.

Table 3.6 shows the number of funded Phase I and Phase II NHLBI SBIR projects, by fiscal year of funding. The research impact of the Great Recession is shown by 0 Phase I awards in FY 2011 and in FY 2012, and then 0 Phase II awards in FY 2011 and only 1 Phase II award in FY 2012. These so called zero award years occurred even though NIH funds were available.

Table 3.6 Number of NHLBI Phase I and Phase II SBIR Funded Projects, by Fiscal Year 2010–2023

Fiscal Year	*Phase I Funded Projects*	*Phase II Funded Projects*
2010	84	32
2011	0	0
2012	0	1
2013	2	6
2014	12	21
2015	60	37
2016	70	45
2017	60	39
2018	77	38
2019	90	40
2020	70	38
2021	71	42
2022	72	44
2023	65	39
	733	422

Source https://www.sbir.gov/sbirsearch/award/all

For the purpose of context, Appendix 1 to this chapter provides an abstract of a representative sample of recently funded Phase I and Phase II projects that are focused on lung and blood issues.[23] A purpose of presenting abstracts of these projects is to illustrate the breadth of research topics that are related to heart disease that are funded by the NHLBI's SBIR program.

Figure 3.7 shows, by fiscal year, the Phase I awards and obligated amounts (1000s) of support for NHLBI projects in current dollars. Figure 3.8 shows, by fiscal year, these amounts (1000s) in constant 2022 dollars ($2022). The trend in both metrics is positive after FY 2012 as shown by the trend lines imposed on both of the figures.

And, Fig. 3.9 shows, by fiscal year, the Phase II award and obligated amounts (1000s) of support for NHLBI projects in current dollars. Figure 3.10 shows, by fiscal year, these amounts (1000s) in constant 2022 dollars ($2022). The trend in both metrics is positive after FY 2012 as shown by the trend lines imposed on both figures.

While NIH Phase I and Phase II funding was available in FY 2011 and in FY 2012, funding for NHLBI SBIR awards was not available (see Table 3.6).

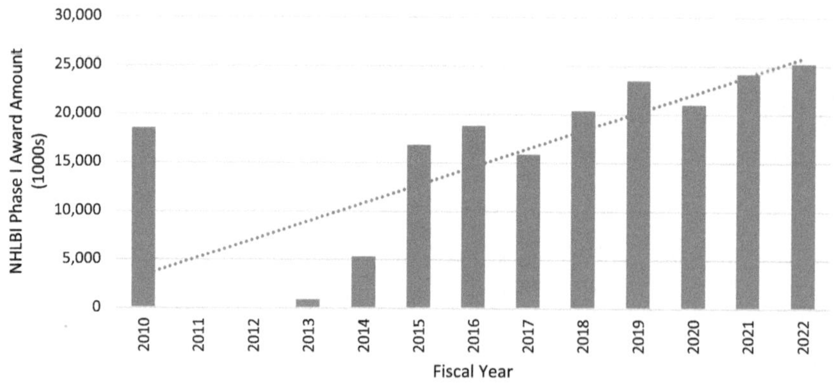

Fig. 3.7 Trend in NHLBI Phase I SBIR Awards and Obligated Amounts, by Fiscal Year (1000s, current dollars) 2010–2022. *Source* https://www.sbir.gov/sbirsearch/award/all. *Note* The trend line was generated through Excel

[23] The abstracts are quoted directly from the noted source.

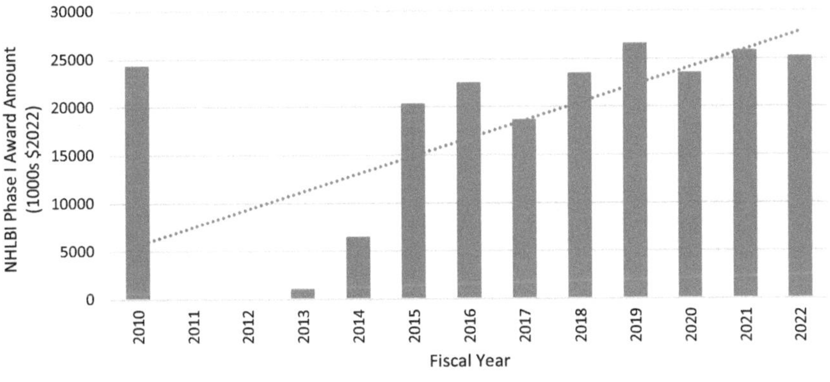

Fig. 3.8 Trend in NHLBI Phase I SBIR Awards and Obligated Amounts, by Fiscal Year (1000s, constant $2022) 2010–2022. *Source* https://www.sbir.gov/sbirsearch/award/all. *Note* The trend line was generated through Excel

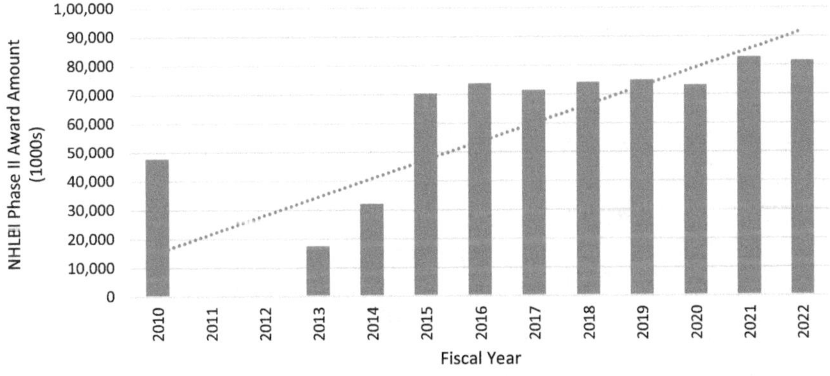

Fig. 3.9 Trend in NHLBI Phase II SBIR Awards and Obligated Amounts, by Fiscal Year (1000s, current dollars) 2010–2022. *Source* https://www.sbir.gov/sbirsearch/award/all. *Note* The trend line was generated through Excel

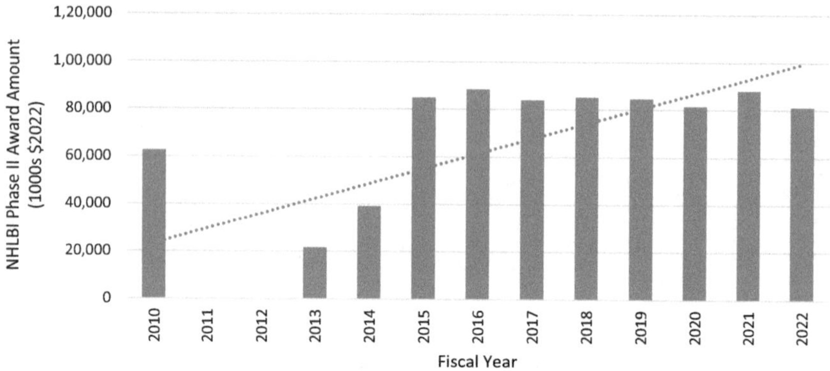

Fig. 3.10 Trend in NHLBI Phase II SBIR Awards and Obligated Amounts, by Fiscal Year (1000s, constant $2022) 2010–2022. *Source* https://www.sbir.gov/sbirsearch/award/all. *Note* The trend line was generated through Excel

Table 3.7 Mean Demographic Characteristics of NHLBI Phase I and Phase II SBIR Funded Firms (in percents) over Fiscal Years 2010–2023

SBIR Program	*Mean Women-Owned Firms*	*Mean Socially and Economically Disadvantaged Firms*
Phase I	11.0%	10.2%
Phase II	7.6%	6.6%

Source https://www.sbir.gov/sbirsearch/award/all

To re-emphasize, the impact of the Great Recession on NHLBI awards is evident from the graphical depictions. There were 0 Phase I awards in FY 2011 and FY 2012. And, there were 0 Phase II awards in FY 2011. However, after an adjustment period of time—an operational adjustment on both the firm applicant's side and the NHLBI administrative side—of about 2 years, the funding levels in current and constant dollars increased.

Table 3.7 shows selective firm level demographic characteristics of the Phase I and Phase II awardees (see the fourth bullet point in the NHLBI SBIR mission and goals statement above). The mean percents, averaged over FY 2010—FY 2023, in the table are relatively small. The mean percent of Phase I awards to a woman-owned firms was 11 % over these years, and the mean percent of Phase I awards to socially and economically disadvantaged firms was 10.2 % over these years. These percents decreased for Phase II awards; 7.6 % of Phase II awards went to woman-owned firms, and 6.6 % of Phase II awards went to socially and economically disadvantaged firms. We will re-visit gender issues in Chap. 6.

The NIH has several in-house programs to support Phase II SBIR research. The Commercialization Readiness Pilot (CRP) Program:[24]

> … provides additional technical assistance and late-stage research and development support not typically covered within small business awards to help products get to market.

Through Small Business Transition Grants, the NIH can support Phase II project mentors to:[25]

> Provide technical and commercial guidance to advance the proposed research project [and]
>
> Support preparing and executing a career development plan to successfully navigate the entrepreneurial process, develop and commercialize products, or operate a small business

These programs help to ensure Phase II project success and thereby enhance both knowledge transfer and technology transfer.

Appendix 1: Recent NHLBI SBIR Phase I and Phase II Projects

Targeting Neutrophil Extracellular Traps for Acute Lung Injury
Acute lung injury (ALI), and its more severe form, acute respiratory distress syndrome (ARDS), are life-threatening conditions with no FDA-approved pharmacologic therapy. More than 200,000 people suffer from ALI/ARDS annually in the US. They are primarily ICU patients who suffer secondary organ injury to the lungs as a result of trauma,

(continued)

[24] See https://seed.nih.gov/small-business-funding/find-funding/crp.

[25] See https://seed.nih.gov/small-business-funding/open-funding-opportunities/small-business-transition-grant.

(continued)

transfusion, burns, infection, sepsis, hemorrhagic shock, smoke inhalation, or oxygen exposure. ALI/ARDS has demonstrated mortality rates as high as 40% as well as significant long-term morbidity. ALI/ARDS pathogenesis is characterized by neutrophilic inflammation and the release of Neutrophil Extracellular Traps (NETs). Neutrolis' founding team has a deep understanding of the biology and pathology caused by NETs. NETs are lattices of high-molecular weight chromatin filaments complexed with toxic proteins. In ALI/ARDS, NETs accumulate in alveolar cavities and capillaries of the lung and prevent blood oxygenation. Neutrolis has developed a lead candidate for therapeutic targeting of NETs. In this research proposal, Neutrolis will generate information on non-clinical properties and formulation of its lead that are required for the pre-IND meeting with the FDA. Specifically, the key outcomes of these aims are to determine the most effective route of administration. Neutrolis will assess an intravenous and inhalational method of drug delivery for treatment of ALI, and characterize their (1) efficacy dose, (2) pharmacological (PK/PD), and (3) toxicological properties. In summary, Neutrolis is well positioned to bring its proprietary developmental lead for treating ALI into the clinic. Given that NETs are abundant in acute and chronic inflammatory diseases, Neutrolis aims to ultimately address the multiplicity of inflammatory conditions, offering hope and relief to millions of suffering patients worldwide

Improved Delivery System for Drug-Coated Balloon Therapy

Atherosclerosis is the leading cause of vascular disease, which accounts for 38% of all deaths in North America. Coronary artery disease is the leading cause of death from atherosclerosis, with over 500,000 deaths per year in the US alone. Peripheral artery disease affects more than 200 million persons worldwide, including at least 8.5 million persons in the United States, and is associated with high rates of cardiovascular events and death as well. Percutaneous intervention via balloon angioplasty is a common treatment for atherosclerosis. We propose to develop a novel angioplasty balloon inflation system to improve the efficacy of drug-coated balloon angioplasty. Atherosclerosis, characterized by the deposition of plaques of fatty material on the inner walls of arteries, can lead to the development of peripheral arterial disease (PAD) due to obstructive narrowing of arteries that supply blood to the extremities. PAD frequently causes a wide variety of ischemic symptoms including pain, non-healing arterial insufficiency ulcers, lower limb tissue loss and gangrene. Percutaneous drug-coated balloon angioplasty of PAD blockages has been observed to reduce symptoms, salvage affected limbs and prolong survival

Development of a Minimally Invasive Partial Circulatory Support Device for Chronic Use

The Nautilus pump is a centrifugal, totally implantable, compact, long-lasting partial circulatory assist device implanted via a minimally invasive pacemaker pocket approach to support LV function for late-stage heart failure intervention. The Nautilus pump will be connected to the systemic circulation by attachment of the pump's inflow port to a cannula placed into the subclavian vein and positioned in the left atrium via a transseptal approach,

(continued)

(continued)

and the outflow port to a vascular graft anastomosed to the subclavian artery. This revolutionary partial support pump is being designed to eliminate the need for invasive techniques to implant full support devices (sternotomy or thoracotomy) and eliminate the need for percutaneous cables and/or drivelines. The Nautilus pump and system will be a minimally invasive, low energy consumption system that will not impose excessive afterload on the LV, therefore maintaining pulsatility. Furthermore, it will retain native heart ventricular muscle integrity, offering the best environment for LV reconditioning. Another feature to be integrated to the pump is the next-generation transcutaneous energy transfer (TET) system, which does not require direct external coil skin contact to power the pump. This is a remarkable feature that is not present in any other competitors' systems. Leveraging pump affinity laws, which govern centrifugal pump performance and are useful to modify pumps for new and different required duties, and the Company's extensive intellectual property portfolio, the Nautilus pump is being designed based on our full support assist pump. It will combine permanent magnetic levitation with a low shear hydrodynamic bearing to produce an ultra-low power consumption pump that still retains the superior blood handling characteristics of full maglev technology. This highly efficient pump is then combined with implantable grade batteries and a light, external mobile wireless power source, making it a totally implanted and wirelessly powered system that does not require a percutaneous driveline, direct skin contact, or bulky external batteries. In-vivo preliminary studies using the full circulatory support pump device validated all the innovative features in this grant proposal, such as a high-efficiency pump with a low hemolysis rate

This SBIR Phase I proposed grant objectives are addressed in two specific aims that will be executed for eight months. In Aim 1, the Nautilus pump will be designed, and a prototype is fabricated to accommodate 2–3 L/min flows at physiologic pressures. In Aim 2, in-vitro studies, using a recirculating blood test loop, will be performed to determine red blood cell hemolysis, platelet and leukocyte activation, vWF degradation, and function, as well as overall blood hemostatic potential, compared to our full circulatory support pump and the BPX-80 Bio Pump™ (Medtronic—Minneapolis, MN, US). The conclusion of the proposed aims will demonstrate the feasibility and hemocompatibility of the Nautilus pump design. It will set the stage for a Phase II SBIR grant application where the performance, safety, and suitability of the device will be evaluated in an in-vivo setting, in addition to the development of a transeptal cannula

Improving Outcomes in Cancer Treatment-Related Cardiotoxicity

Anthracyclines, such as Doxorubicin (DOX), are effective for the treatment of many cancers (Ovarian, Multiple Myeloma, Kaposi Sarcoma, Leukemia, Bone Sarcoma, Breast, Endometrial, Gastric, Liver, Kidney, and other Cancers). The global DOX market is increasing annually and expected to reach $1.3B by 2026. DOX toxicity is therefore relevant to a broad number of cancers. However, chemotherapy induced cardiac toxicity has substantial morbidity and mortality. Cardiotoxicity and recovery from DNA damaging chemotherapy is dose-dependent. With cancer survivors estimated at 19 million in the USA

(continued)

(continued)

by 2025, Dox-induced cardiotoxicity is considered to be a part of the "cardio-oncology epidemic". The development of new approaches to reduce chemotherapy-induced cardiotoxicity is essential. Dexrazoxane (Dex), is FDA approved for the specific indication of "doxorubicin administration in women with metastatic breast cancer who have received a cumulative doxorubicin dose of 300 mg/m2 and who will continue to receive doxorubicin therapy to maintain tumor control". Dex has the risk of myelotoxicity. In off label use of Dex in other cancer populations, cardiac protection was incomplete. In the pediatric population Dex provided "'incomplete acute cardioprotection and "no impact on chronic cardioprotection or overall survival". LightSeed has assembled a highly experienced team (oncologist-cancer biologist (with prior biotechnology company expertise), cardio-oncologist, high throughput lead discovery expert, immune cancer biologist- mouse geneticist) in order to identify and repurpose FDA-approved compounds with "dual function" (enhance cancer cell killing by DOX but protection from DOX cardiotoxicity). Three compounds from the FDA approved compound library have been validated. We are seeking additional "dual function" compounds from the libraries. We have deployed an innovative genetically modified murine testing system which: (i). allows comparison with the incumbent technology (Dex), (ii). provides a normal immune system for the tumor immune response. (iii). allows analysis of the host immune response using double knockin fluoresecent reporter genes. (iv). allows detection of the tumor growth using a third fluorescent report gene for in vivo progression analysis. LightSeed will identify additional "dual function" compounds by high throughput screening under the direction of a core director who is highly experienced with HTS screening (previously head of Lead Discovery at Janssen for 15 yrs). LightSeed will use cardiomyocyte cells derived from pooled iPSC-CM (iPSC-derived cardiomyocytes) and cancer cells. This proposal will: (SA1). Screen a library that consists of FDA and EU approved compounds, using an assay that protects human cardiac myocytes from DOX-induced cardiac toxicity and enhances cancer cell killing. (SA2). Validate these compounds in tissue culture and (SA3) in a novel "dual function" reporter mouse system

Improving Anticoagulation Monitoring in Pediatric Patients: Use of a Microfluidic Platform to Test Low Volume Blood Samples Obtained by Heel-Stick Collection

Children treated for congenital heart defects or other disorders of hypercoagulation are prescribed unfractionated heparin (UFH) or low molecular weight heparin (LMWH) throughout surgical treatment; they may be prescribed heparin for up to 2 weeks post-surgery to prevent thrombosis. UFH is a fiscally efficient, effective anticoagulant that should be closely monitored over time to ensure proper dosage and patient response; LMWH is a newer anticoagulant that is gaining traction among cardiologists. Despite the need for constant monitoring of heparin levels, sometimes every 4 hours, there are limitations to currently available systems hindering delivery of optimal heparin level results to physicians. These barriers include individual assays that use relatively large volumes of blood (~2 mL per assay) and long turnaround times between measurements (up to 2 hours) that limit the utility of these tests for appropriate dosing, especially in the beginning

(continued)

(continued)

of anticoagulation therapy. In addition, commonly utilized assays (partial thromboplastin time (PTT), activated PTT (aPTT), and prothrombin time) show poor correlation to heparin levels infused in patients, but are still in use due to their historical value and wide adoption in the field. More rapid and accurate methods are needed to assess heparin levels that reduce the overall amount of blood and provide physicians with sufficient dosing information to deliver optimal therapy to pediatric patients. Through a previously funded NIH Fast-Track project, we developed a novel and scalable platform to assess and monitor heparin therapy administered to pediatric patients through measurement of Factor Xa (FXa) and Anti- thrombin III (ATIII) levels. In response to input from key opinion leaders, we are developing a third assay for aPTT. This assay panel is run on our near-patient digital microfluidic (DMF) platform using 50 mL of whole blood input. The fluorescent assays use nanoliter volumes of sample and reagents on a disposable single-use cartridge. Although the platform has been developed and feasibility has been demonstrated with the assays, much work remains for this product to be commercially ready. Funding through this Commercialization Readiness Pilot (CRP) will support studies to establish reliable reagent and cartridge manufacturing processes, preclinical studies to validate the manufacturing processes, and development of the FDA regulatory strategy for a full multi-site clinical method comparison study. Our approach is strengthened by our continued partnership with Boston Children's Hospital, the high potential clinical impact of the tests, and thorough analysis and global distributor relationships demonstrating a significant market gap. The DMF heparin monitoring product will fill a critical gap in pediatric care by providing an inexpensive rapid, low-blood volume system for comprehensive assessment of heparin levels in a hospital or clinic setting. The successful completion of these CRP aims will accelerate commercial development so that we are poised to immediately complete final validation studies for regulatory approval and commercial

Development of a Low Dose Clinical Lung Screening Prototype for Early Detection of COPD and Lung Cancer Using a Novel X-ray Source to Enable Talbot-Lau Interferometry

Chronic obstructive pulmonary disease (COPD) and lung cancer are the third and sixth most common causes of death worldwide. One major challenge is that there are no effective screening methods capable of early detection of these diseases and when these diseases are finally detected, they are often at advanced stages for which few effective treatment strategies exist. In the case of lung cancer, more than half of people die within the year of diagnosis. Darkfield (scattering-based) x-ray contrast has been recently demonstrated to provide exciting capabilities for early detection of lung pathologies, including cancer and COPD at doses comparable to conventional chest radiography. This contrast mechanism differs significantly from current approaches, which use the absorption of x-rays for contrast rather than the scattering of x-rays. Accessing information provided by this contrast mechanism requires an emerging grating-based x-ray technique called Talbot-Lau interferometry, which uses three sets of gratings (source, phase, and detector) to achieve contrast. However, a critical bottleneck for using this technique at the high x-ray

(continued)

(continued)

energies (~60 keV) required for imaging through a human chest is a source grating with the aspect ratios required cannot be fabricated. We propose to develop a lung darkfield imaging prototype using a major x-ray source innovation that removes the need for the x-ray source grating to enable Talbot-Lau interferometry at high x-ray energies. The system will critically enable demonstrations of the clinical potential of darkfield radiography for early detection of lung pathologies. The proposed Phase I 6-month project is a proof-of -principle of a grating-less Talbot-Lau breadboard set-up on a phantom. The proposed Phase II 24-month project is to develop a complete prototype system and experimentally verify its performance

Novel Strategies to Clear Bacteria from the CF Lung

Cystic fibrosis (CF) is a genetic disease caused by mutations in the cystic fibrosis transmembrane regulator (CFTR) gene. CF airways are immunocompromised and become colonized with bacteria soon after birth. Chronic bacterial infection leads to persistent and severe neutrophil-dominated pulmonary inflammation, high lung protease levels, lung damage and a decline in FEV1. CFTR modulator/correctors from Vertex such as TRIKAFTA significantly increase CF patient lung function by rt10% but do not bring it into the normal range and for patients with pre-existing bacterial lung infections, do not clear bacteria from their lungs. Moreover, these compounds do not treat CF patients with nonsense mutations where no CFTR protein is produced. Thus, there is a critical unmet need for novel, CFTR mutation-agnostic therapies to help clear bacteria from CF lungs and limit neutrophilic lung damage. Short Palate LUng and Nasal epithelial Clone 1 (SPLUNC1) is a secreted protein that is highly expressed in the lung, where it plays a key role in maintaining lung health. SPLUNC1 is a CF gene modifier, and patients with reduced SPLUNC1 levels have lower FEV1 and exacerbate more frequently. Orai1 is a ubiquitously expressed plasma membrane Ca2+ channel that regulates inflammation. We found that SPLUNC1 inhibits Orai1. However, SPLUNC1 is rapidly degraded by neutrophil elastase (NE), which we posit results in greater Orai1 activity and more inflammation. Consistent with this, our preliminary data indicate that Orai1 is upregulated in CF patient lung immune cells. Given Orai1's proximal role in the immune response, Orai1 is thus an attractive target whose inhibition is predicted to help resolve CF inflammation. Eldec Pharma has developed a robust, novel peptidomimetic called ELD607, which reprises SPLUNC1's ability to inhibit Orai1, yet is significantly more stable in the presence of NE, and significantly more potent/efficacious. ELD607 is stable in proteolytic CF sputum, and inhibits Ca2+-influx in freshly-isolated CF patient peripheral neutrophils and in CF sputum-derived immune cells in a mutation-agnostic fashion. In murine lung infection models with common CF pathogens including P. aeruginosa and S. aureus, a single, inhaled dose of ELD607 reduced lung inflammation (neutrophilia, cytokines, NE) by 90%, decreased lung bacterial infection by 3-4 log10 CFUs and increased survival. In a chronic CF model (SCNN1B mice), ELD607 reduced neutrophilia and increased survival. These experiments demonstrate that rebalancing the lung's inflammatory response by inhibiting Orai1 enhances the lungs' natural ability to clear

(continued)

(continued)

pathogens. In this proposal, we will use wild-type and CF mice to understand which immune effector cells are regulated by ELD607. The CF ferret model developed by Dr Engelhardt and coworkers at the University of Iowa spontaneously develops chronic CF lung disease including inflammation and bacterial infection. We will first validate that we can deliver sufficient doses of ELD607 via nebulizer to safely inhibit Orai1 in wild-type and CF ferret lungs. Then we will chronically administer ELD607 to CF ferrets with existing lung disease in order to study the impact of ELD607 on CF disease progression

ViTrack: Wearable, Accurate, Continuous Blood Pressure Monitor to Improve Outcomes in Hypertensive Diseases of Pregnancy

Dynocardia, a Tufts University School of Medicine and Massachusetts Institute of Technology spinoff, is addressing an unmet need for real-world accurate and continuous non-invasive blood pressure (BP) and other cardio-hemodynamic parameters. ViTrack™, a unique optomechanical sensor and computer vision technology, is the first to measure beat-to-beat systolic (SBP) and diastolic BPs (DBP) in real-world settings with the accuracy of invasive arterial pressure without external calibration, irrespective of subject movement or wrist position relative to the heart (hydrostatic pressure change). Dynocardia is expanding into the hospital market and exploring its technology's potential in other areas of healthcare, particularly in maternal health. Dynocardia has secured an SBIR Phase II grant [Project Number: 1R44HL167356-01] to study the effectiveness of ViTrack technology in ensuring the safety and well-being of mothers and their children during pregnancy. ViTrack's beat-to-beat accurate measurements, irrespective of patient movement or wrist level to the heart, provide the patient's circadian BP pattern, including 24-hr mean BP, nighttime BP, and BP variability (BPV). In addition, ViTrack also measures heart rate, respiratory parameters, and advanced hemodynamics. The hypertensive diseases of pregnancy (HDP) are a significant cause of morbidity and mortality. The current standard for measuring BP in pregnant women is the periodic use of oscillometric arm-cuff devices. The oscillometric devices indirectly estimate SBP and DBP based on artery wall oscillations during cuff deflation. Measurement errors inherent to this indirect method, patient posture/movement, and wrong cuff size lead to unreliable BP measurements in 50% of routine office visits. Oscillometric device errors are compounded in pregnant women due to hemodynamic and vascular changes that reduce oscillations of the arterial wall, resulting in BP underestimation. In contrast, these hemodynamic changes will have less impact on ViTrack measurements because it utilizes pressure-dependent spatiotemporal skin displacement to measure SBP and DBP directly. In addition, random clinic measurements during antenatal visits lead to a 30% wrong diagnosis of HDP due to white coat or masked hypertension. In addition, there is a need for remote and continuous accurate measurement of BP for prediction and early deduction of preeclampsia. The circadian BP parameters, such as 24-hr mean SBP, nighttime BP, and BPV, are better predictors of preeclampsia than clinic BP measurements. ViTrack, the first standalone, wearable, connected device, can provide remote, accurate circadian BP data for correct

(continued)

(continued)

diagnosis and enable predictive monitoring for better outcomes. In preclinical, outpatient [vs. auscultatory method], and inpatient [vs. invasive arterial pressure], ViTrack met FDA standards for accuracy. In this SBIR Phase II study, we are expanding the application of ViTrack in HDP in partnership with NYC Health + Hospitals that serves underserved populations, a large percentage of them non-Hispanic Black population at high risk for HDP. The Aims of the study are: Specific Aim (SA) 1: Assess the accuracy of ViTrack BP measurements (n=48). SA1(a): Determine the accuracy of ViTrack measurements in pregnant women (n=33) as per the European Society of Hypertension International Protocol-2010) [34]; SA1(b): Determine accuracy in severe preeclampsia (n=15), defined as BP measurement of 170/10 or more and proteinuria of 500 mg or more in 24-hr. Milestone: ViTrack accurately measures BP in pregnant women, including women with severe preeclampsia. SA2: Assessment of 24-hr BP with ViTrack (n=100). Collect 24-hr BP with ViTrack and intermittent cuff BP measurements as per standard practice from the contralateral arm; SA2(a): Assess tolerability/usability and reliability of 24-hr beat-to-beat BP in unconstrained subjects (n=20); SA2(b): Compare the 24-hr BP profile in pregnant women with and without HDP (n=80); SA2(c): Compare the number of hypotensive/hypertensive episodes with ViTrack continuous measurements vs. the intermittent cuff measurements. Milestone: ViTrack provides reliable 24-hr data despite patient movement. The data generated will validate ViTrack as the first standalone technology for accurate and continuous BP during pregnancy. This foundational data will inform the commercial build, final clinical validation and FDA submission, and 510(k) approval for continuous BP measurement in pregnant women. In addition, further randomized control trials will validate the application of ViTrack in risk prediction, early diagnosis, and management of preeclampsia and, thus, as the new standard of care for BP monitoring during pregnancy

Source https://www.sbir.gov/sbirsearch/award/all

References

Link, A. N. 2023. The US Small Business Technology Transfer (STTR) program: An assessment and an evaluation of the program. *Annals of Science and Technology Policy* 7:81–151.

Link, A. N. 2024. Small firm research supported by the National Institutes of Health's National Cancer Institute. *Annals of Science and Technology Policy* 8:300–366.

Link, A. N., and A. C. O'Connor. 2025. *Small business innovation in the public interest: A study of the US National Institutes of Health.* Cheltenham, UK and Northampton, MA, USA: Edward Elgar Publishing.

CHAPTER 4

The NHLBI SBIR Database

Abstract The empirical analysis in this book comes from Phase II National Heart, Lung, and Blood Institute (NHLBI) Small Business Innovation Research (SBIR) program project data collected by the National Research Council (NRC) within the National Academies of Sciences, Engineering, and Medicine. The project data relate to fiscal years 1992 through 2001. The survey is described in this chapter, and tables are presented on various characteristics of the funded NHLBI projects. Emphasis is given to Phase II projects that were successful, that is, projects that did not have their research projects fail.

4.1 The NRC Survey

In anticipation of the 2008 reauthorization of the SBIR program,[1] the US Congress charged the National Research Council (NRC),[2] within the National Academies of Sciences, Engineering, and Medicine, through the

[1] See Link and Van Hasselt (2023) for a more complete legislative history of the re-authorization of the SBIR program.

[2] "The National Research Council (NRC) is the operating arm of the United States National Academies of Sciences, Engineering, and Medicine and is overseen by a governing board that consists councilors from each of the three Academies. The National Academies of Sciences, Engineering, and Medicine are private, nonprofit institutions that provide expert advice on

A. N. Link, A. C. O'Connor, *The Economics of Heart Disease Research*, Palgrave Advances in the Economics of Innovation and Technology,
https://doi.org/10.1007/978-3-032-13547-6_4

Small Business Innovation Research Program Reauthorization Act of 2000 (Public Law 106–554) (NRC, 2008, p. 13), to conduct:

> … a comprehensive study of how the SBIR program has stimulated technological innovation and used small businesses to meet federal research and development needs … and [to] make recommendations on improvements to the program.

As a part of its study, the NRC administered a survey in 2005 to a representative sample of the National Institutes of Health (NIH) funded Phase II Small Business Innovation Research (SBIR) projects conducted by the firms that had previously received a Phase II award.[3] The survey-based information was codified into what we call the 2005 NRC database. Among the 495 NIH-funded Phase II project firms that responded to the NRC Phase II SBIR survey questions, in total or in part, 64 of the awarded Phase II projects were funded through the National Heart, Lung, and Blood Institute's (NHLBI's) SBIR program.[4]

The NHLBI data in the 2005 NRC database that are considered descriptively in the following chapters of this book only relate to Phase II project awards over the fiscal years (FYs) 1992 through 2001.

Table 4.1 reports the number of NHLBI Phase II projects in the NHLBI SBIR database, by fiscal year of funding. Over the fiscal years of funding, the number of Phase II projects in the NHLBI SBIR database increased after fiscal year 1998.

some of the most pressing challenges facing the nation and world. Their work helps shape sound policies, inform public opinion, and advance the pursuit of science, engineering, and medicine." See https://tethys.pnnl.gov/organization/national-research-council-national-academies-nrc.

[3] The NRC also collected survey information from a random sample of Phase II awarded firms funded through the Department of Defense, the Department of Energy, the National Aeronautics and Space Administration, and the National Science Foundation. These data formed the NRC database. See Link and O'Connor (2025).

[4] In the sample, each of the 64 Phase II projects is associated with a unique firm. That is, each firm in the sample had one Phase II project. Although not directly relevant to this book, for completeness we note that the Congress again charged the NRC to study the SBIR program through the Continued Evaluation of the National Academy of Sciences section of the National Defense Authorization Act for Fiscal Year 2012 (Public Law 112–81). Unfortunately, data collected through the accompanying NRC study of the SBIR program do not allow for a disaggregation of NIH Phase II project information by Institute or Center.

Table 4.1 Number of Phase II Projects in the NHLBI SBIR Database, by Fiscal Year of Funding (n = 64) 1992–2001

Fiscal Year of the Phase II Project Funding	*Number of Phase II Projects*
1992	2
1993	3
1994	3
1995	2
1996	4
1997	7
1998	6
1999	16
2000	8
2001	13
	64

Source NHLBI SBIR database

Table 4.2 Total NHLBI Phase II SBIR Awards in Current Dollars and Constant Dollars, by Fiscal Year of Funding (n = 64) 1992–2001

Fiscal Year of Phase II Funding	*Phase II Award (1000s, $current)*	*Phase II Award (1000s, $2022)*
1992 (n = 2)	$870.3	$1,697
1993 (n = 3)	$1,494	$2,845
1994 (n = 3)	$1,411	$2,631
1995 (n = 2)	$1,314	$2,400
1996 (n = 4)	$2,864	$5,137
1997 (n = 7)	$5,228	$9,218
1998 (n = 6)	$4,026	$7,021
1999 (n = 16)	$12,201	$20,979
2000 (n = 8)	$6,436	$10,822
2001 (n = 13)	$5,042	$8,291
	$40,886	$71,041

Source NHLBI SBIR database. *Note* Current dollar Phase II awards are concerted to constant dollar ($2022) amounts using the Gross Domestic Product (GDP) annual deflator

Table 4.2 reports the total funding levels of the Phase II projects in the NHLBI SBIR database, by fiscal year, in current dollars and in constant

Table 4.3 Mean NHLBI Phase II SBIR Awards in Constant Dollars ($2022), by Fiscal Year of Funding (n = 64) 1992–2001

Fiscal Year of Phase II Funding	*Mean Phase II Award (1000s, $2022)*
1992 (n = 2)	$849
1993 (n = 3)	$948
1994 (n = 3)	$877
1995 (n = 2)	$1,200
1996 (n = 4)	$1,284
1997 (n = 7)	$1,317
1998 (n = 6)	$1,170
1999 (n = 16)	$1,331
2000 (n = 8)	$1,353
2001 (n = 13)	$638

Source NHLBI SBIR database. *Note* Constant dollar ($2022) amounts using the Gross Domestic Product (GDP) annual deflator

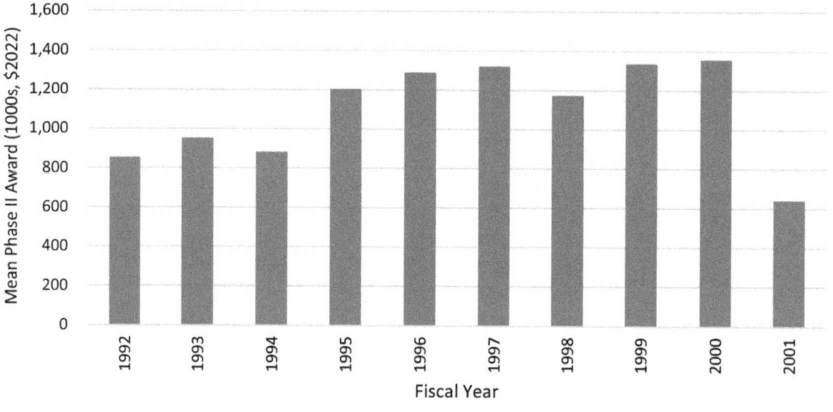

Fig. 4.1 Trend in the Mean NHLBI Phase II SBIR Awards ($2022), by Fiscal Year of Funding (n = 64) 1992–2001. *Source* NHLBI SBIR database

2022 dollars. Table 4.3 reports the mean constant dollar level of funding of the Phase II projects by fiscal year. Related to Table 4.3, Fig. 4.1 shows the trend in the mean level of award funding ($2022) by fiscal year of funding. The decline in the mean level of funding in FY 2021 perhaps reflects the effects of the Covid-19 pandemic on the research capabilities of

Table 4.4 Geographic Distribution of NHLBI Phase II SBIR Awards Across States (n = 64)

State (alphabetical)	*Number of Phase II Projects*	*Percent of Phase II Awards*
Alabama	1	1.55%
California	7	11.56%
Connecticut	1	1.82%
Delaware	1	1.80%
Florida	1	1.97%
Georgia	1	1.15%
Illinois	3	3.88%
Iowa	1	1.83%
Maine	1	1.90%
Maryland	4	6.02%
Massachusetts	9	14.75%
Michigan	5	6.86%
Minnesota	2	3.56%
Missouri	1	1.71%
New York	5	8.00%
North Carolina	2	1.80%
Oregon	1	1.83%
Pennsylvania	5	6.68%
Rhode Island	1	2.23%
Texas	2	3.04%
Utah	2	2.91%
Virginia	5	7.41%
Washington	2	3.66%
Wisconsin	1	2.08%
	64	100%

Source NHLBI SBIR database

firms; the research laboratories in many firms were partially or fully closed during the pandemic. Thus, the extent of research proposed by a firm for a Phase II project was perhaps limited.

Regarding the geographic distribution of funded NHLBI Phase II projects, the surveyed projects in the NHLBI SBIR database were located in 24 states, as shown in Table 4.4. The largest number of awards went to firms in Massachusetts (9 Phase II awards accounting for 14.06% of the Phase II award amounts) followed by California (7 Phase II awards accounting for 10.94% of the Phase II award amounts).

Table 4.5 Status of NHLBI SBIR Phase II SBIR Projects (n = 64)

Status	*Number of Phase II Projects*
Phase II project was not yet completed	6
Phase II project was discontinued	21
Phase II project was completed	37
	64

Source NHLBI SBIR database. *Note* Project status is as of the time of the 2005 NRC survey

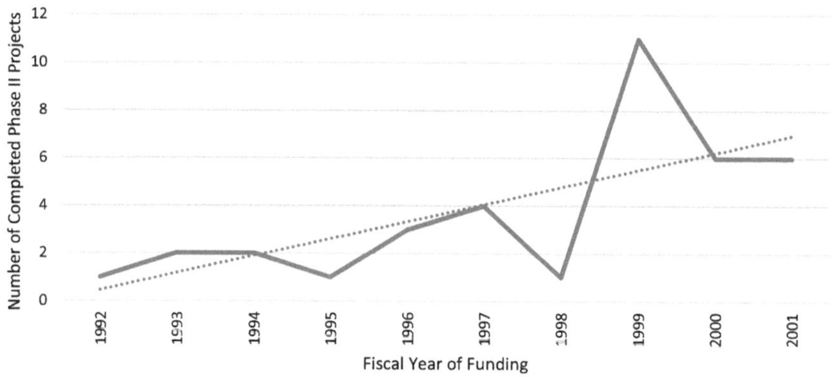

Fig. 4.2 Number of Completed NHLBI Funded Phase II SBIR Projects, by Fiscal Year of Funding (n = 37) 1992–2001. *Source* NHLBI SBIR database. The trend line was generated by Excel

Finally, the status of the 64 Phase II projects at the time of the 2005 NRC survey is shown in Table 4.5. These status categories are discussed in Chap. 5 in terms of which Phase II projects were included in (or excluded from) any related descriptive analysis.

Finally, Fig. 4.2 shows the upward trend in the number of completed Phase II projects (n = 37), by fiscal year of funding. Note that the number of completed Phase II projects in the Covid-19-affected FY 2021 was below trend.

4.2 Another Look at Discontinued Projects

Reported in Table 4.5 is information that 21 of the 64 NHLBI-funded Phase II SBIR projects failed in the sense that they were discontinued prior to completing the proposed Phase II SBIR research project. This table also reports that 6 of the 64 Phase II projects had not yet (as of survey year 2005) been completed. In this section of the chapter, we focus on the 21 failed projects.

Boyce (2023), among others, has studied failed SBIR research projects. He concluded the following from his review of the extant literature (2023, pp. 104–106):

> The literature examining the determinants of SBIR project failure is limited ... [H]aving university faculty involved in the R&D project translate[s] to a relatively large reduction in the probability a project failed ...

Figure 4.3 shows the number of failed Phase II projects by fiscal year of funding (n = 21), keeping in mind that a Phase II project is generally designed to be a two-year project and that there were at least four years between the year of Phase II project funding and the 2005 NRC survey. One should not interpret Fig. 4.3 as being a representative sample of failed Phase

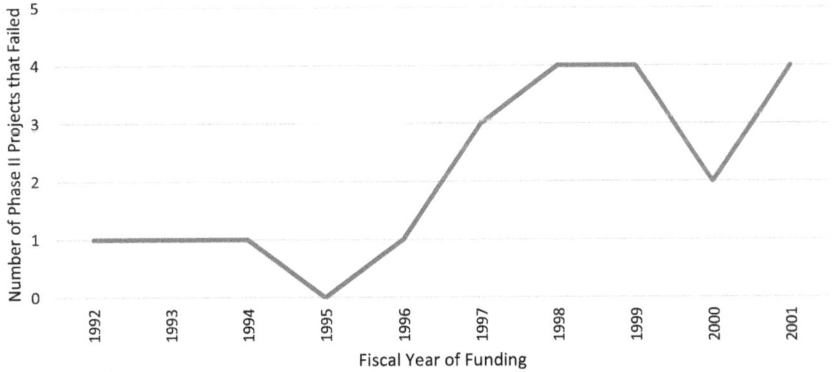

Fig. 4.3 Number of Failed NHLBI Funded Phase II SBIR Projects, by Fiscal Year of Funding (n = 21) 1992–2001. *Source* NHLBI SBIR database

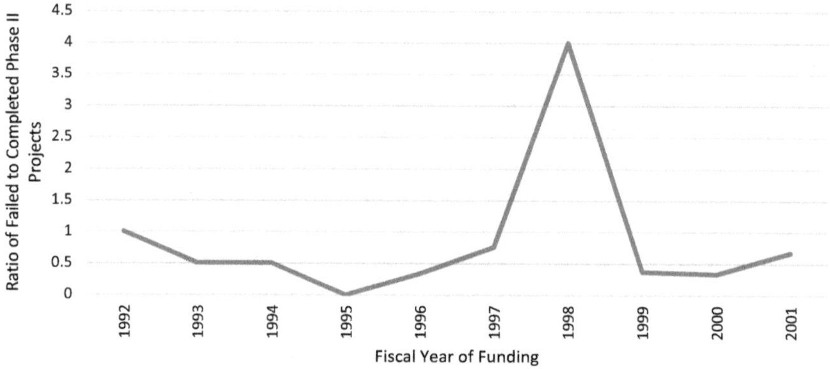

Fig. 4.4 Ratio of Failed NHLBI Funded Phase II SBIR Projects to Completed NHLBI Funded Phase II SBIR Projects, by Fiscal Year of Funding (n = 58) 1992–2001. *Source* NHLBI SBIR database. *Note* Six of the 64 NHLBI-funded Phase II projects were not completed; hence n = 58 in the table title

Table 4.6 Failed and Completed NHLBI Funded Phase II Projects with University Relationships

	Failed Projects (n = 21)	*Completed Projects (n = 35)*
Percent of Phase II projects with a university relationship	52.4%	68.6%

Source NHLBI SBIR database. *Note* Six of the 64 NHLBI-funded Phase II Projects were not completed. Two of the 37 firms with completed projects did not respond to the survey question about university relationships

II SBIR projects by funding year. Rather, it is only a characterization of the 21 failed NHLBI Phase II-funded SBIR projects in the NRC database.

And, Figure 4.4 shows the ratio of failed to completed Phase II projects by fiscal year of funding. Noticeably, the large increase in this ratio is in FY 1998. But, as emphasized above, this figure should also not be interpreted as being a representative sample of all NHLBI Phase II SBIR projects.

Building on the empirical findings by Boyce (2023) and the to be discussed role of external human capital inflows from a university in Chap. 6, of the 21 failed Phase II projects, 52.4% (11 of 21 projects)

Table 4.7 Failed and Completed NHLBI Funded Phase II Projects with Patents and with Scientific Papers Published

	Failed Projects (n = 21)	*Completed Projects (n = 35)*
Patents received per Phase II project	0.62	1.23
Scientific papers published per Phase II project	0.67	5.74

Source NHLBI SBIR database. *Note* Six of the 64 NHLBI-Funded Phase II Projects were not completed

had a university relationship and of the 37 completed Phase II projects, 64.9% (24 of 37 projects) had a university relationship.[5] The descriptive evidence in Table 4.6 is not at odds with the Boyce finding.

Regarding the 21 failed Phase II projects collectively, 13 patents were awarded to the Phase II projects, and 14 scientific papers were published. On a per project basis, 0.62 patents were received per failed projects and 0.67 scientific papers were published per failed project. In comparison to the 37 completed Phase II projects, collectively across all projects, 43 patents were awarded to 37 firm projects, and those firm projects published 201 scientific papers. On a per-project basis for the completed projects, 1.23 patents were received per completed projects and 5.74 scientific papers were published per completed project. Even when an NHLBI-funded Phase II project fails and thus does not commercialize, it still makes a knowledge transfer contribution to society. See Table 4.7.

In the following Chap. 5, information from the NHLBI SBIR database is used to describe knowledge transfer metrics from the NHLBI.

References

Boyce, M. 2023. *Principal investigators and R&D failure: Probability of innovation failure in small business.* Cham, Switzerland: Springer.

[5] The 24 Phase II project that has a university relationship of some type responded in the affirmative to the NRC survey question: "In executing this award, was there any involvement by universities faculty, graduate students, and/or university developed technologies?"

Link, A. N., and A. C. O'Connor. 2025. *Small business innovation in the public interest: A study of the US national institutes of health*. Cheltenham, UK and Northampton, MA, USA: Edward Elgar Publishing.
Link, A. N., and M. Van Hasselt. 2023. *Small firms and US technology policy: Social benefits of the US small business innovation research program*. Cheltenham, UK and Northampton, MA, USA: Edward Elgar Publishing.

CHAPTER 5

Knowledge Transfer Metrics from the NHLBI SBIR Survey

Abstract This chapter introduces 25 alternative knowledge transfer metrics based on the NHLBI database of Phase II awards. These metrics are categorized as knowledge outflow metrics, knowledge inflow metrics, and two-way knowledge flow metrics. Descriptive statistics are provided for each metric. Four metrics are emphasized and are graphically illustrated in terms of firm employment and Phase II award amounts: licensing agreements, patents received, scientific papers published, and commercialization rates.

5.1 The Portfolio of Metrics

The National Research Council (NRC) Small Business Innovation Research (SBIR) survey addressed what we are referring to in this book as knowledge transfer channels and metrics, although the phrase *knowledge transfer* was not used in the NRC survey instrument. The 25 knowledge transfer metrics considered in the NRC survey, based on our own categorizations, are listed in Table 5.1 along with the associated NRC survey questions.

Table 5.2 groups the 25 NRC knowledge transfer metrics into three directional-flow categories: those that represent a knowledge outflow from the Phase II SBIR project, those that represent a knowledge inflow to enhance the Phase II project, and those that represent a two-way flow of knowledge from and to the Phase II project.

A. N. Link, A. C. O'Connor, *The Economics of Heart Disease Research*, Palgrave Advances in the Economics of Innovation and Technology,
https://doi.org/10.1007/978-3-032-13547-6_5

Table 5.1 NHLBI Knowledge Transfer Metrics

Metric	*NRC Survey Question (paraphrased)*
Commercialization	Has your company and/or licensee had any actual sales of products, processes, services or other sales incorporating the technology developed during this project?
Private-sector sales	To date, approximately what percent of total sales from the technology developed during this project went to the private sector?
DOD sales	To date, approximately what percent of total sales from the technology developed during this project went to the Department of Defense (DOD)?
NIH sales	To date, approximately what percent of total sales from the technology developed during this project went to the NIH (National Institutes of Health)?
State or local government sales	To date, approximately what percent of total sales from the technology developed during this project went to the state or local government?
Export market sales	To date, approximately what percent of total sales from the technology developed during this project went to the export market?
Licensing agreement	As a result of the technology developed during this project, did your company engage in a licensing agreement with other companies and investors?
Sale of company	As a result of the technology developed during this project, was your company sold to another company or to investors?
Partial sale of company	As a result of the technology developed during this project, was your company partially sold to another company or to investors?
Sale of technology rights	As a result of the technology developed during this project, did your company sell technology rights to other companies and investors?
Company merger	As a result of the technology developed during this project, did your company merge with other companies and investors?
Joint venture agreement	As a result of the technology developed during this project, did your company engage in a joint venture agreement with other companies and investors?
Marketing/ distribution agreement	As a result of the technology developed during this project, did your company engage a marketing or distribution agreement with other companies and investors?
Manufacturing agreement	As a result of the technology developed during this project, did your company engage in a manufacturing agreement with other companies and investors?

(continued)

Table 5.1 (continued)

Metric	*NRC Survey Question (paraphrased)*
R&D agreement	As a result of the technology developed during this project, did your company engage in an R&D agreement with other companies and investors?
Customer alliance	As a result of the technology developed during this project, did your company engage in a consumer alliance with other companies and investors?
Hired employees	Number of current employees who were hired as a result of the technology developed during this Phase II project.
Retained employees	Number of current employees who were retained as a result of the technology developed during this Phase II project
Patents received	Please give the number of patents received from the technology developed as a result of this Phase II project.
Copyrights received	Please give the number of copyrights received from the technology developed as a result of this Phase II project.
Trademarks received	Please give the number of trademarks received from the technology developed as a result of this Phase II project.
Scientific papers published	Please give the number of scientific papers published from the technology developed as a result of this Phase II project.
University involvement	Did your company have a relationship with any university or college?
University human capital	Did your company have a relationship with any university or college that involved the use of faculty or graduate students in the Phase II project?
University technical capital	Did your company have a relationship with any university or college that involved the use of university technology in the Phase II project?

Note In the NRC survey and in this book, the words *firm, business*, and *company* are used interchangeably

Our categorical listing in Table 5.2 illustrates dimensions of the heterogeneity of knowledge; not only the heterogeneity of sources of knowledge (internal versus external sources) but also the heterogeneity of the structure of knowledge (human capital versus technical capital). Although it is beyond the scope of this book (and beyond the scope of the data in hand), a further taxonomy of knowledge could reveal that some knowledge is tacit and some knowledge is codified.[1]

[1] Audretsch and Link (2019) also describe other heterogeneous characterizations of knowledge: incremental versus radical knowledge, specialized versus diversified knowledge, and basic versus applied knowledge.

Table 5.2 Directional Transfer of Knowledge Metrics Associated with the NHLBI Phase II Projects

Knowledge Outflow	*Knowledge Inflow*	*Two Way Knowledge Flow*
Commercialization	Hired employees	Company merger
Private-sector sales	Retained employees	Joint venture agreement
DOD sales	University technical capital	Marketing/distribution agreement
NIH sales		Manufacturing agreement
State or local government sales		R&D agreement
Export market sales		Customer alliance
Licensing agreement		University involvement
Sale of company		University human capital
Partial sale of company		
Sale of technology rights		
Patents received*		
Copyrights received*		
Trademarks received*		
Scientific papers published		

Source 2005 NRC survey
* Potential knowledge outflow

As explained by Audretsch and Link (2019, p. 32), ideas are themselves a source for knowledge:

> Ideas that are codified generally are agreed upon and can be articulated and written down ... By contrast, ideas on which there is not general agreement and that cannot be articulated in a coherent written form are generally characterized as being tacit in nature.[2]

A characteristic of surveys in general—and the NRC survey is no exception—is that not all of the invited respondents actually respond to each survey question. Not surprisingly, this was the case with the NRC survey-based metrics reported in Tables 5.3, 5.4, and 5.5 which are related to the knowledge transfer metrics related to the outflow, inflow, and two-way flow of knowledge, respectively. The number (n) of Phase II projects used for the calculations in Tables 5.3, 5.4, and 5.5 relates only to those firms for which

[2] According to Antonelli (2014, p. 235): "knowledge tacitness implies that dedicated interactions among agents are necessary to make its use possible."

Table 5.3 NHLBI Knowledge Outflow Metrics

Metric	*n*	*Mean*	*Range*	*Comment*
Commercialization	37	0.432	0/1	Commercialization = 1 if the firm reported any product, process, service, or other sales; 0 otherwise
Commercialization	35	0.429	0/1	
Private-sector sales	16	65.31	0–100	Non-responses to the survey questions about the source of sales (private-sector, DOD, NIH, state or local government, and export market) might reasonably be interpreted as having 0%
DOD sales	16	1.25	0–15	
NIH sales	16	2.19	0–20	
State or local government sales	16	0.94	0–15	
Export market sales	16	12.81	0–70	
Licensing agreement	37	0.324	0/1	Licensing, sale of company, partial sale of company, and sale of technology rights include finalized and negotiated US and foreign relationships
Licensing agreement	35	0.314	0/1	
Sale of company	37	0.081	0/1	
Partial sale of company	37	0.054	0/1	
Sale of technology rights	37	0.108	0/1	
Patents received*	35	1.23	0–11	Patents, copyrights, trademarks, and scientific publications are count variables
Copyrights received*	35	0.48	0–8	
Trademarks received*	35	0.54	0–2	
Scientific papers published	35	5.74	0–75	

Source NHLBI SBIR database

Table 5.4 NHLBI Knowledge Inflow Metrics

Metric	*n*	*Mean*	*Range*	*Comment*
Hired employees	35	5.80	0–140	Employees are a count variable
Retained employees	35	1.771	0–8	
University technical capital	24	0.417	0/1	Equipment as well as licensed technology

Source NHLBI SBIR database

the Phase II project was completed (n = 37; see Table 4.5) and for which the surveyed firms actually responded to the survey question.

For each metric presented in these tables, descriptive statistics are reported and comments about the metrics are offered. In some instances, a respondent might have skipped (i.e., left blank) a response opportunity

Table 5.5 NHLBI Two-Way Knowledge Flow Metrics

Metric	*n*	*Mean*	*Range*	*Comment*
Company merger	37	0.054	0/1	Mergers, joint venture agreements, marketing/distribution agreements, manufacturing agreements, R&D agreements, and customer alliances include finalized and negotiated US and foreign relationships
Joint venture agreement	37	0.135	0/1	
Marketing/ distribution agreement	37	0.270	0/1	
Marketing/ distribution agreement	35	0.286	0/1	
Manufacturing agreement	37	0.108	0/1	
R&D agreement	37	0.189	0/1	
R&D agreement	35	0.200	0/1	
Customer alliance	37	0.081	0/1	
University involvement	24	0.875	0/1	Human or technical capital involvement
University human capital	24	0.708	0/1	Faculty or graduate student involvement
University technical capital	24	0.417	0/1	Technology involvement

Source NHLBI SBIR database

to a survey question because he or she did not know the accurate response (e.g., number of employees at a particular date in the past) to a survey question. In other instances, a respondent's non-response might have been intended to be an implied zero response (e.g., the percent of sales to a specific agency). The numerical responses in Tables 5.3, 5.4, and 5.5 only reflect actual responses; we did not assume that a missing value had an implied response, likely of zero.

In Table 5.3 we report descriptive statistics on commercialization for both n = 37 and n = 35 (n = 35 is explained below), and we do the same for licensing arrangements. We note that n = 35 for patents received and for scientific papers published (data were not available for all of the n = 37 Phase II project responses).

Regarding the knowledge outflow metrics in Table 5.3, several observations are offered under the column heading of Comments. Regarding commercialization, when it comes to identifying the percentage of sales of the developed technologies sold as a product, process, or service, the

NHLBI SBIR database is sparse on detailed information. Information on the consumer of the Phase II SBIR project technology is available for only 16 Phase II projects. Among those 16 Phase II projects, the location of consumers is predominantly the private sector, likely in the health care or related industries, or so we speculate; following private sector sales are sales in the export market.

Among the knowledge outflow metrics that are most closely aligned with technology transfer metrics—especially those technology transfer metrics most frequently focused on in the United States—are licensing agreements, patents received, and scientific papers published. On average (n = 35), 31.4% of the Phase II projects were involved in a licensing agreement. The number of scientific papers published (mean = 5.74; n = 35) dominated numerically when compared to the number of patents received (1.23; n = 35). Perhaps, the review process for patent applications at the US Patent and Trademark Office (USPTO) is longer than the review process for scientific papers submitted to academic journal outlets.

Knowledge from other sources that flow into the SBIR funded firm's project take numerous forms but only a few of those can be quantified using the NHLBI SBIR database. Knowledge can come into the SBIR-funded firm though new employees who are hired to be part of the Phase II project, some of whom are retained. And, knowledge can come into the firm through the use of technical capital from a university or college. As shown in Table 5.4, on average nearly 6 new employees were hired to work on a funded Phase II project, and nearly one-third of those employees were on average retained by the firm when the Phase II project was completed. Of the 24 Phase II projects that responded to the survey question about the use of technical capital from a university, 41.7% relied on that inflow of technical knowledge to complete their Phase II projects.

As shown in Table 5.5, there are what we refer to as two-way sources of knowledge flows meaning that a firm was involved not only in bringing new knowledge inside, but also there is the possibility that internal knowledge could, in turn, be shared externally. Of the network relationships that were most often reported in the NHLBI SBIR database, marketing/distribution agreements were the most common (28.6% of projects so engaged, n = 35) followed by research and development (R&D) agreements (20.0% of projects so engaged, n = 35).[3] Of the 24 firms that

[3] For example, an R&D agreement involves the open sharing of technical knowledge by all parties involved.

responded to the survey question about its Phase II project having a university relationship, 70.8% reported that they incorporated university human capital into the conduct of their Phase II SBIR research compared to only 41.7% incorporating university technical capital.

5.2 A Knowledge Production Function

As we wrote in Chap. 3, the mission and goals of the National Institutes of Health (NIH) Small Business Innovation Research (SBIR) program are generally similar to the mission and goals of the SBIR program in general:[4]

- Stimulate technological innovation;
- Meet federal research and development needs;
- Increase private sector commercialization of innovations developed through federal R&D [research and development] funding; and
- Foster and encourage participation in innovation and entrepreneurship by socially and economically disadvantaged (SDB) persons and women-owned small businesses (WOSB).

In this section of the chapter, we explore the association between the mission and goals of the NIH SBIR program and appropriate knowledge transfer metrics. Where possible, we draw inferences from our findings.

The NIH SBIR mission and goals are not necessarily independent of each other. For example, an increase in private sector commercialization (the third bullet above) can stimulate technological innovations (the first bullet above) in other organizations through the spillover of knowledge embodied in a commercialized product, process, or service. As well, encouraging the participation of disadvantaged persons and women-owned small businesses increases the potential supply of new technology-based products, processes, and services, which in turn stimulates technological innovations.

The structural model that we use for the following discussion of knowledge transfers and empirical description of those transfers is referred to in the literature by the phrase ***knowledge production function***. In this model,

[4] See https://seed.nih.gov/small-business-funding/small-business-program-basics/understanding-sbir-sttr.

which is posited for an economic unit, knowledge outflow innovation (*I*) is assumed to be related to the stock and flow of knowledge (*Kn*) as:[5]

$$I = \mathrm{f}(Kn) \tag{5.1}$$

A, if not the, critical question to ask about the model presented as equation 5.1 is: Where does *Kn* originate? As one might infer from the discussion above, an economic unit's endowment of knowledge comes from internal (subscript *i*) resources, be they in the form of human capital or technical capital, as well as from external (subscript *e*) resources, be they also in the form of human capital or technical capital. And, these sources of knowledge can take the form of stocks as well as flows.

Thus, we consider, for an economic unit, be it a firm or even a firm's research project, two functional representations of *Kn*:

$$Kn = \mathrm{f}(HC_i, TC_i) \tag{5.2}$$

and

$$Kn = \mathrm{f}(HC_e, TC_e) \tag{5.3}$$

where HC_i represents the stock of internal human capital, TC_i represents the stock of internal technical capital; HC_e represents the inflow of the stock of external human capital, and TC_e represents the inflow of the stock of external technical capital. It follows then that:

$$I = \mathrm{f}(HC_i, TC_i) \tag{5.4}$$

and

$$I = \mathrm{f}(HC_e, TC_e) \tag{5.5}$$

where the function form represented by f (·) might vary across equations 5.2 through 5.5. We will explore the model represented by equation 5.4 in

[5] This formulation is motivated by Griliches (1979) and was built on by Audretsch and Link (2019).

this chapter, and we will re-visit the model represented as equation 5.5 in Chap. 6.[6]

The following discussion is structured in a manner to parallel the mission and goals of the SBIR program listed above and listed below in italics.

Stimulate Technological Innovation: Technological innovation (I), as referred to in the mission and goals of the NHLBI SBIR program, can be stimulated in general though knowledge transfers (Kn). Here, we explore covariates—HC_i and TC_i (and HC_e and TC_e in Chap. 6)—with innovation, I, from the model in equation 5.4.

Following the model represented as equations 5.4, I is measured in terms of the binary variable of licensing agreements (*Licenses*), and I is also measured in terms of the count variables of number of patents received (*Patents*) and number of scientific papers published (*Publications*). Given the paucity of non-zero observations on the other technology transfer metrics metrics available in the NHLBI SBIR database—for example, Sale of company, Partial sale of company, Sale of technology rights, Copyrights received, and Trademarks received—only the above three knowledge outflow innovation (I) metrics are considered. And, based on the specifications of equations 5.4, the covariates considered are the stock of internal human capital (HC_i) in the form of employees and internal technical capital (TC_i) in the form of the Phase II research award. Descriptive statistics on these variables are in Table 5.6 (n = 35).[7]

The nine descriptive figures that immediately follow—Fig. 5.1 through Fig. 5.9—illustrate relationships between the stock of internal human capital (HC_i) and three of the four knowledge outflow innovation metrics, and they illustrate the relationship between the stock of internal technical capital (TC_i) and the same three knowledge outflow innovation metrics as above. The stock of internal human capital variable is the number of employees in the firm at the time the Phase II proposal was submitted to the NHLBI SBIR program (*ProposalEmp*).

The stock of internal technical capital variable is the inflation adjusted to year 2022 ($2022) amount (adjusted using the Gross Domestic Product (GDP) Deflator) of the Phase II award (*PhaseIIAward*).

[6] One could correctly argue that the more relevant model would be $I = f(HC_i, TC_i, HC_e, TC_e)$, but the data in the NHLBI database are limited in project observations and thus such a model would not be empirically supported.

[7] The variable *Commercial* is discussed below.

Table 5.6 Variables for the Estimation of Equation 5.4 Using Knowledge Outflow Metrics (n = 35)

Variable (number of observations)	*Mean*	*Standard Deviation*	*Range*
Knowledge Outflow Metrics			
Licensing	0.314	0.471	0/1
Patenting	1.23	2.756	0–11
Publishing	5.74	12.885	0–75
Commercial	0.429	0.502	0/1
Covariates			
ProposalEmp	8.86	12.852	1–68
PhaseIIAward	$1185	377.87	$601—$2649
PhaseIIAwardperEmp	$241.85	246.41	$7.44—$1282

Source NHLBI SBIR database
Notes Employees (*Emp*) is the number of employees in the firm at the time the Phase II proposal was submitted
PhaseIIAward is the amount of the Phase II awards at the time the Phase II project was funded, in thousands, adjusted for inflation by the GDP deflator ($2022). *PhaseIIAwardperEmp* if the ration of the latter to the former

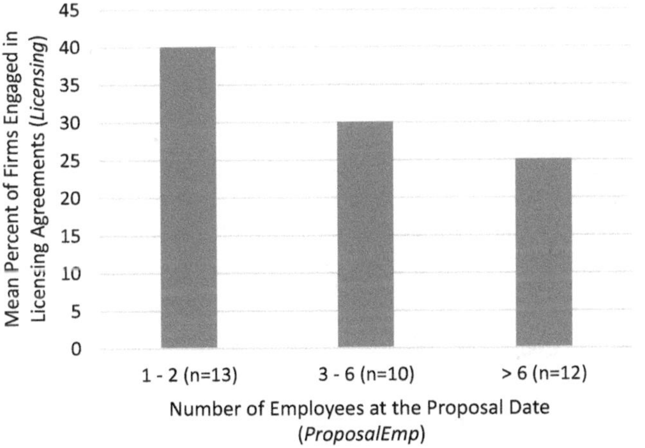

Fig. 5.1 Licensing Agreements by Employment Size (n = 35). *Source* NHLBI SBIR database

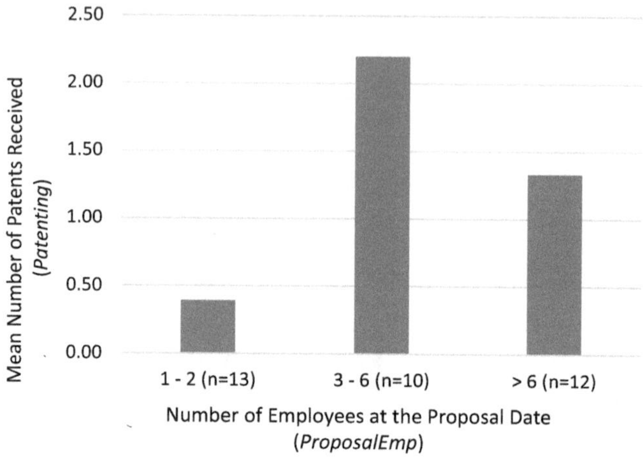

Fig. 5.2 Patents Received by Employment Size (n = 35). *Source* NHLBI SBIR database

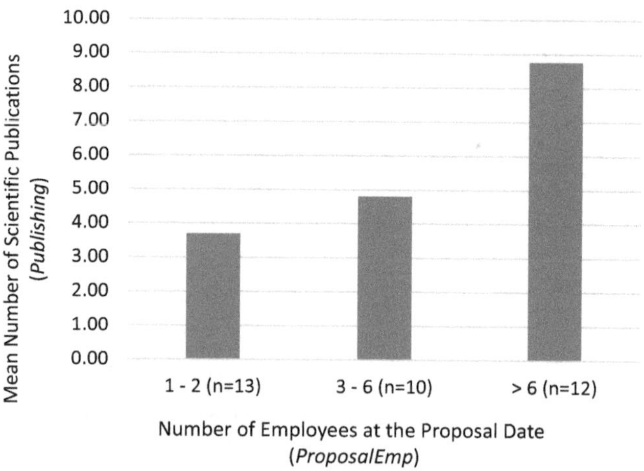

Fig. 5.3 Scientific Papers Published by Employment Size (n = 35). *Source* NHLBI SBIR database

Another internal technical capital variable incorporates aspects of both internal human capital and internal technical capital. That variable is the ratio of *PhaseIIAward* to (*ProposalEmp* + *HiredEmp*) measured as the stock of internal technical capital per current and newly hired employees (*PhaseIIAwardperEmp*).

In each of the following nine figures, the project data are categorized into three or four groups of approximately the same size (measured in different ways). We adopted this descriptive graphical approach for each of these relationships because of the relatively small number of NHLBI Phase II SBIR projects in the NHLBI SBIR database (n = 64), but only 37 of the 64 projects completed their Phase II project. The operative number of observations is however n = 35 due to non-responses to certain survey questions.

Figure 5.1 shows that the mean percent of firms that are engaged in licensing agreements (*Licensing*) decreases over increasing categories of employment size (*ProposalEmp*). Figure 5.2 shows a non-linear relationship between the mean number of patents received (*Patenting*) and increasing categories of employment size. Finally, Fig. 5.3 shows an increasing relationship between the mean number of scientific papers published (*Publishing*) and categories of employment size. Thus, to generalize, firm size measured in terms of *ProposalEmp* is negatively related to *Licensing* and positively related to *Publishing*.

Figure 5.4 shows that *Licensing* initially decreases over increasing categories of the amount of the Phase II award (*PhaseIIAward*), and then it dramatically increases. *Patenting* also decreases abruptly over increasing categories of the amount of the Phase II award, but then it increases slightly as shown in Fig. 5.5. *Publishing* does the same as *Patenting*, but more smoothly; see Fig. 5.6. In other words, the size of the Phase II award is generally negatively related to *Patenting* and *Publishing*.

Figures 5.7, 5.8, and 5.9 are not based on a single internal metric, but rather they are based on the amount of the Phase II award per employee (*PhaseIIAwardperEmp*). Over this metric, there is no clear increasing or decreasing pattern across the metrics of *Licensing* and *Patenting*. *Publishing* is decreasing over these Phase II award amounts per employee, but not smoothly.

While informative, the model represented as equation 5.4 and the descriptive analysis of the model in Figs. 5.1 through 5.9 are structured under the implicit assumption that the three outflow variables that approximate dimensions of knowledge outflow innovations are independent

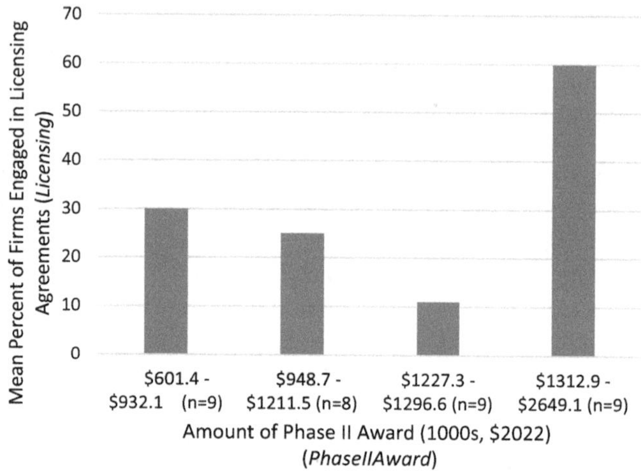

Fig. 5.4 Licensing Agreements by Phase II Award Amount (1000s, $2022) (n = 35). *Source* NHLBI SBIR database

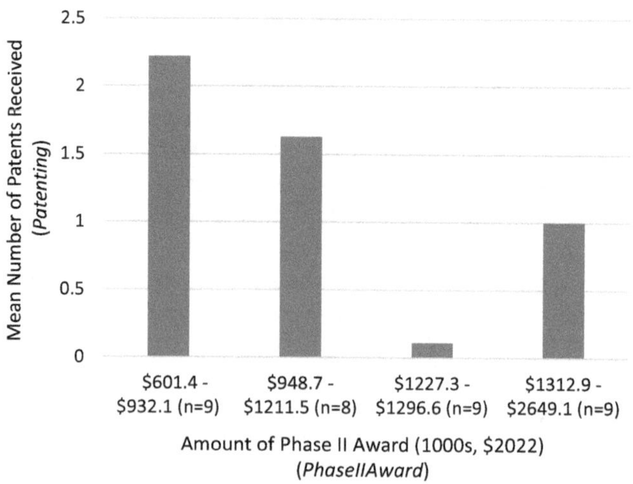

Fig. 5.5 Patents Received by Phase II Award Amount (1000s, $2022) (n = 35). *Source* NHLBI SBIR database

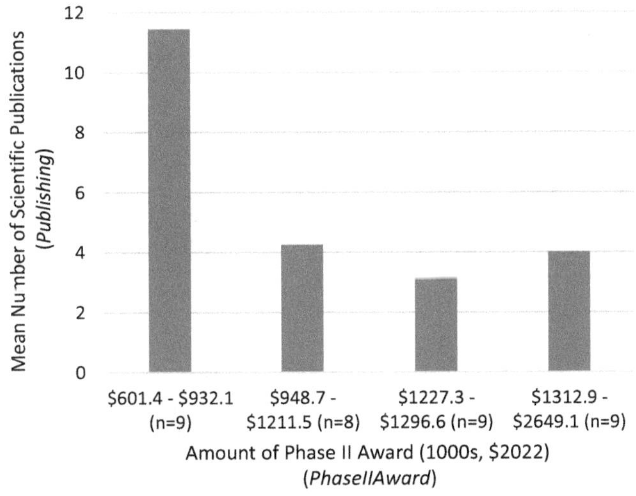

Fig. 5.6 Scientific Papers Published by Phase II Award Amount (1000s, $2022) (n = 35). *Source* NHLBI SBIR database

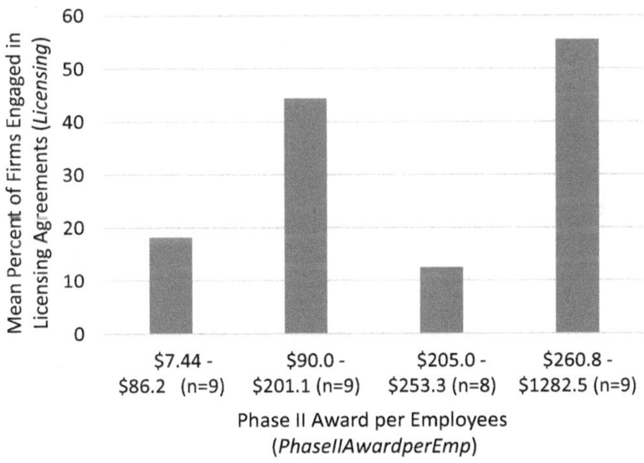

Fig. 5.7 Licensing Agreements by Phase II Award Amount (1000s, $2022) per Employees (n = 35). *Source* NHLBI SBIR database

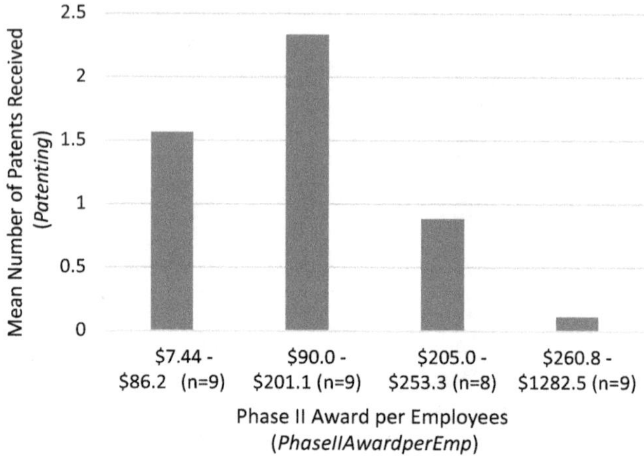

Fig. 5.8 Patents Received by Phase II Award Amount (1000s, $2022) per Employees (n = 35). *Source* NHLBI SBIR database

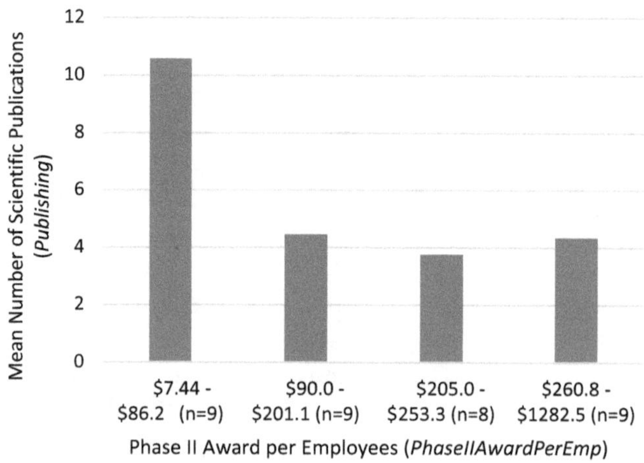

Fig. 5.9 Scientific Papers Published by Phase II Award Amount (1000s, $2022) per Employees (n = 35). *Source* NHLBI SBIR database

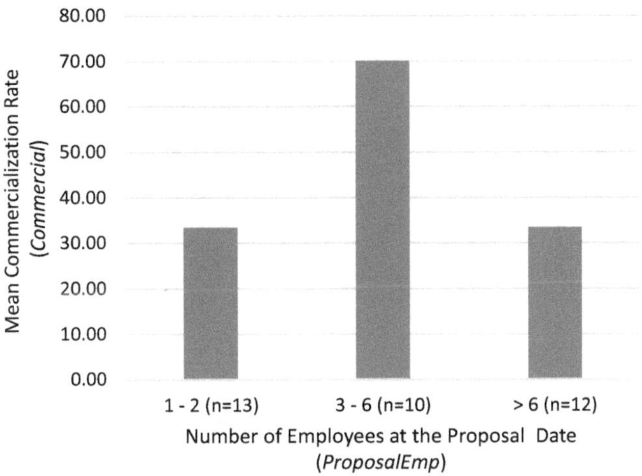

Fig. 5.10 Commercialization Rate by Employment Size (n = 35). *Source* NHLBI SBIR database

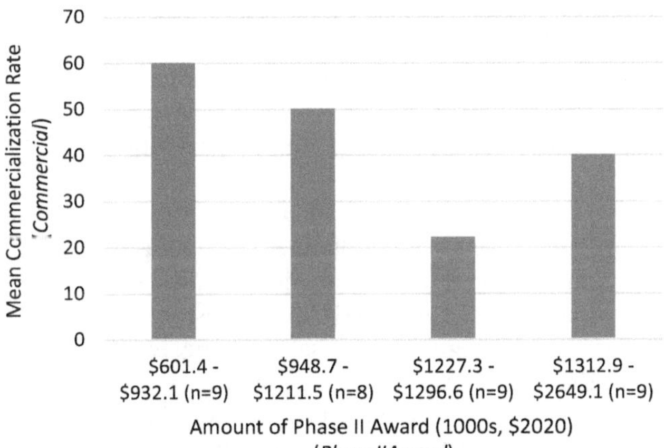

Fig. 5.11 Commercialization Rate by Phase II Award Amount (1000s, $2022) (n = 35). *Source* NHLBI SBIR database

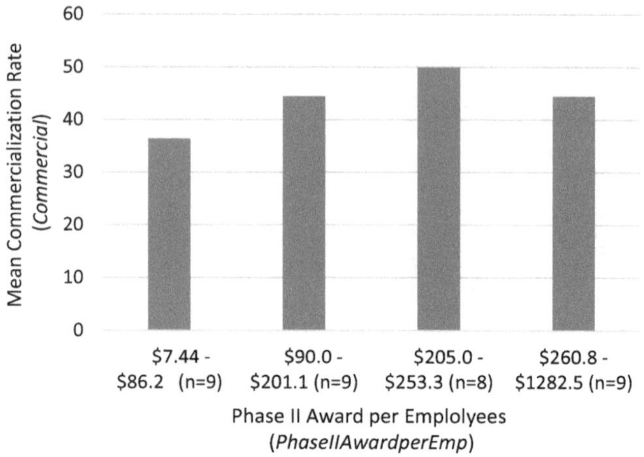

Fig. 5.12 Commercialization Rate by Phase II Award Amount (1000s, \$2022) per Employees (n = 35). *Source* NHLBI SBIR database

of each other. However, they may not be. For example, the correlation coefficient between *Licensing* and *Publishing* is 0.295 ($p = 0.086$) and the correlation coefficient between *Patenting* and *Publishing* is 0.638 ($p < 0.0001$).[8] Were there more Phase II SBIR project observations in the NHLBI SBIR database than n = 35, we could have considered a revision of equation 5.4 in which the dependent innovation variables were a portfolio of metrics.

Meet Federal Research and Development Needs: The NHLBI SBIR database is rich in the sense that it contains (paraphrasing from Table 5.1) information about the percent of total sales from the technology developed during this project that have gone to [federal] customers. Specifically, we are interested in the percentage of total sales to the Department of Defense (DOD) and to the NIH because they are the only two agencies for which the survey questions are related.[9] Because the number of Phase II observations is small (n = 16, of which 14 responses were 0), we simply report in this

[8] See Hayter and Link (2018) for a theoretical explanation of this relationship.

[9] While the mission and goals of the NIH SBIR program are explicit about federal research and development needs, Table 5.3 (n = 16) shows that the largest percent of sale is to private-sector firms and organizations (65.31%) followed by sales to the export market (12.81%).

subsection that the mean percentage of sales to DOD by the 2 non-zero percent projects is 10%, and the mean percent of sales to NIH by the 2 non-zero percent projects is 18.5%.

Increase Private Sector Commercialization: Information in the NHLBI SBIR database allows for the construction of a binary commercialization variable (*Commercial*) as defined by the survey question reported in Tables 5.1 and 5.3. Also reported in Table 5.3 is a commercialization rate (n = 37) of 43.2% and a commercialization rate (n = 35) of 42.9%. Figures 5.10 through 5.12 summarize the rate of commercialization by the same three or four categorical measures used in the figures above for n = 35.

There is at least one notable pattern in these three figures. That pattern is that there is not a consistent increasing or decreasing relationship between *Commercial* and any of the HC_i or TC_i knowledge stock metrics, although there is a suggestive pattern of an increasing relationship between *Commercial* and the amount of the Phae II award per employee. Not shown in these three figures is the following. The commercialization variable, *Commercial*, from Phase II SBIR projects is positively correlated with the number of scientific papers published (*Publishing*) from the Phase II project. The correlation coefficient is 0.290 ($p = 0.090$).

Foster and Encourage Participation in Innovation and Entrepreneurship: The enabling legislation for the SBIR program discussed in Chap. 3 does not define the verbs to *foster* or to *encourage* in the mission and goals statement: "Foster and encourage participation in innovation and entrepreneurship by socially and economically disadvantaged persons and women-owned small businesses." And, there is no information in the NHLBI SBIR database from which one might infer dimensions of the meaning of to *foster* or to *encourage*. Thus, we simply illustrate in Table 5.7 the number of firms conducting Phase II research by alternative ownership characteristics of gender. The projects being considered in this chapter

Table 5.7 Woman-Owned and Minority-Owned Firms Conducting Phase II Projects (n = 35)

Ownership Characteristic	*Number of Firms Conducting Phase II Projects*
Woman Owned	5
Minority Owned	1

Source NHLBI SBIR database

are predominately owned by while males. Only 5 of 35 Phase II projects are owned by a woman, and only 1 of 35 Phase II projects is minority owned.

5.3 Summary

Table 5.8 summarizes the descriptive findings presented in Fig. 5.1 through 5.9 in terms of *Licensing*, *Patenting*, and *Publishing*. Three patterns were shown in the figures and are shown in the table. One, the mean percent of Phase II proposals that are involved in licensing agreements decreases with firm size measured in terms of the number of employees in the firm at the time of the Phase II SBIR proposal. Two, the mean number of scientific papers published increases with firm size measured in terms of the number of employees in the firm at the time of the Phase II SBIR proposal. And three, there is a general decreasing pattern of publishing by the amount of the Phase II award and by the amount of the Phase II award per employee. Regarding *Commercial*, there are non-linear patterns in mean values across the categories of number of employees, the amount of the Phase II award (1000s, $2022), and the amount of the Phase II award per employee.

Table 5.8 Summary of *Licensing*, *Patenting*, *Publishing*, *Commercial*, by Alternative Categories of Funded Firms (n = 35)

Categories	*Licensing*	*Patenting*	*Publishing*	*Commercial*
ProposalEmp				
1–2 (n = 13)	38.4%*	0.38	3.69	30.8%
3–6 (n = 10)	30.0%	2.20	4.80	100%
>6 (n = 12)	25.0%	1.33	8.75	33.3%
PhaseIIAward				
$601.4—$932.1 (n = 9)	33.3%	2.22	11.44	55.6%
$948.7—$1211.5 (n = 8)	25.0%	1.63	4.25	50.0%
$1227.3—$1296.6 (n = 9)	11.1%	0.11	3.11	22.2%
$1312.9—$2649.1 (n = 9)	55.6%	1.00	4.00	44.4%
PhaseIIAwardperEmp				
$7.44—$86.2 (n = 9)	11/1%	1.56	10.56	33.3%
$90.0—$201.1 (n = 9)	44.4%	2.33	4.44	44.4%
$205.0—$253.3 (n = 8)	12.5%	0.88	3.38	50.0%
$260.0—$1282.5 (n = 9)	55.6%	0.11	4.33	44.4%

Source NHLBI SBIR database

* For interpretative purposes, 38.4% of the 13 firms with 1 or 2 employees at the time the Phase II proposal was submitted were engaged during their Phase II project is licensing agreements

References

Antonelli, C. 2014. Dynamics of knowledge governance. In *Routledge handbook of the economics of knowledge*, eds. C. Antonelli and A. N. Link, 232–262. London: Routledge.

Audretsch, D. B., and A. N. Link Link. 2019. *Sources of knowledge and entrepreneurial behavior.* Toronto: University of Toronto Press.

Griliches, Z. 1979. Issues in assessing the contribution of research and development to productivity growth. *The Bell Journal of Economics* 10:92–116.

Hayter, C. S., and A. N. Link. 2018. Why do knowledge-intensive entrepreneurial firms publish their innovative ideas? *Academy of Management Perspectives* 32:141–155.

CHAPTER 6

Characteristics of Knowledge Transfers from the NHLBI SBIR Research

Abstract Various characteristics associated with knowledge transfers are discussed in this chapter. The characteristics emphasized are the gender of the owner of the firm conducting the Phase II research. Also, the use of external university-based human capital and technical are discussed. These characteristics are shown through the use of graphical analysis to be related to the innovation outputs of licensing, patenting, publishing, and commercialization in varying degrees.

6.1 Gender and Innovative Behavior

There is a rich academic and policy literature related to gender and the innovative behavior of firms. As one example, Link and Morrison (2019, p. 93) concluded their survey of woman-owned (and minority-owned) firms that had previously conducted Phase II Small Business Innovation Research (SBIR) projects with the following observations:

> Our empirical findings, which represent a contribution to the relevant literature, from our all-agency analyses, with agency controls as regressors, are:
>
> - A Phase II research project is more likely to be discontinued or to fail in businesses that are minority owned compared to businesses that are not minority owned.

A. N. Link, A. C. O'Connor, *The Economics of Heart Disease Research*, Palgrave Advances in the Economics of Innovation and Technology,
https://doi.org/10.1007/978-3-032-13547-6_6

- There is no evidence that the probability of a project being discontinued or failing varies by the gender of the business owner.
- The probability of commercialization does not vary by either the minority status or gender status of the business.
- Men-owned businesses are more successful in the marketplace with their commercialized technology than are women-owned businesses.
- Minority-owned businesses are more patent active than white-owned businesses.
- Women-owned businesses are less patent active than men-owned businesses.
- There is no evidence that minority ownership or gender ownership affects publication activity.

While some of the Link and Morrison (2019) findings are not directly relevant to the analysis of National Health, Lung, and Blood Institute (NHLBI) Phase II SBIR projects, those findings that are relevant merit a discussion in this chapter.

Figures 6.1 through 6.4 describe the three knowledge outflow innovation metrics and one knowledge outflow performance metric previously discussed in Chap. 5, keeping in mind that the number of Phase II SBIR

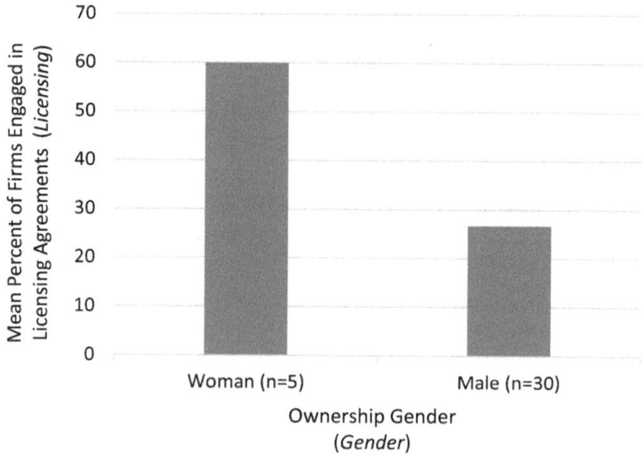

Fig. 6.1 Licensing Agreements by Ownership Gender (n = 35). *Source* NHLBI SBIR database

projects in firms owned by women is only 5 compared to 30 Phase II SBIR projects in firms owned by men. These descriptive figures, Figs. 6.1 through 6.4, show differences in each knowledge outflow variable from Phase II SBIR projects between women-owned and men-owned firms. But, because of the limited number of firms in the NHLBI SBIR database that were owned by women, any generalization from the descriptive finding below should only be made with care and with qualifications that the differences do not necessarily relate to other Institutes within the National Institutes of Health (NIH).

Link and Morrison (2019) did not consider systematically licensing activities. Figure 6.1 shows that women-owned firms are licensing active than men-owned firms.

Our findings about gender for the NHLBI Phase II SBIR-funded firms and their projects are somewhat comparable to the findings discussed by Link and Morrison (2019) who used a large sample of Phase II SBIR projects from five agencies one of which was the NIH, in the aggregate. Link and Morrison (2019) found that women-owned firms across the five agencies patent less from their Phase II SBIR projects than men-owned firms. We also find that women-owned firms funded through the NHLBI SBIR program (n = 5) received fewer patents from their Phase II projects than men-owned firms (n = 30); a mean of 1.4 patents received by men-owned firms compared to a mean of 0.20 patents received by women-owned firms. See Fig. 6.2.

Link and Morrison (2019) also found no difference in publishing activity between women-owned firms and men-owned firms. Our findings are not at odds with the Link and Morrison findings in this regard; a mean of 6 scholarly publications for women-owned firms (n = 5) compared to a mean of 5.7 scholarly publications for men-owned firms (n = 30). See Fig. 6.3.

Finally, Link and Morrison (2019) found that the probability of commercialization from a Phase II SBIR project does not vary by ownership gender. In contrast, we find that the probability of commercialization from an NHLBI Phase II project is, on average, 20 percentage points greater for women-owned firms (60% probability of commercialization; n = 5) compared to men-owned firms (40% probability of commercialization; n = 30). See Fig. 6.4.

See also the summary data in Table 6.1.

In the following section, we describe differences in the knowledge outflow innovation metrics and the knowledge outflow performance

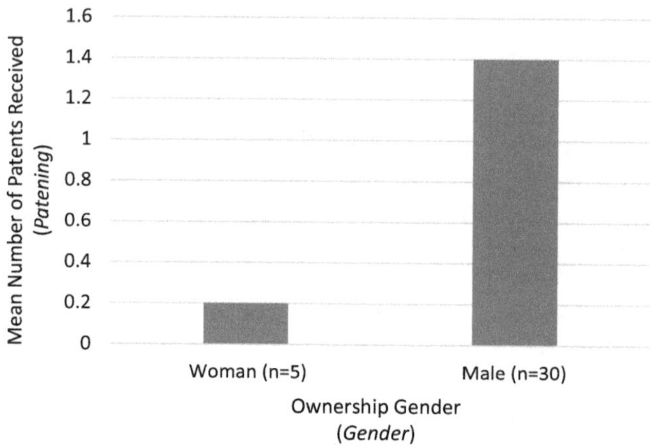

Fig. 6.2 Patents Received by Ownership Gender (n = 35). *Source* NHLBI SBIR database

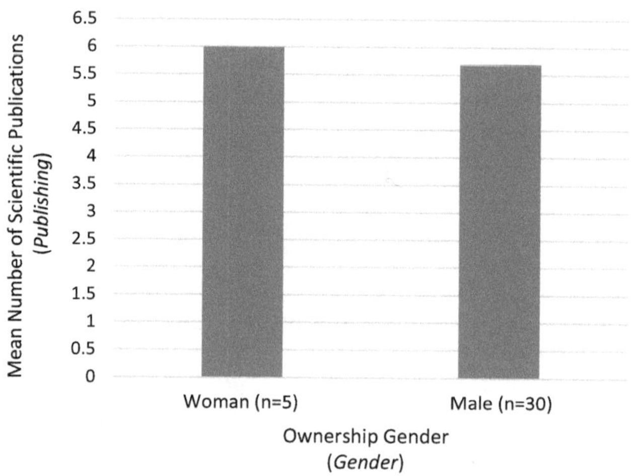

Fig. 6.3 Scientific Papers Published by Ownership Gender (n = 35). *Source* NHLBI SBIR database

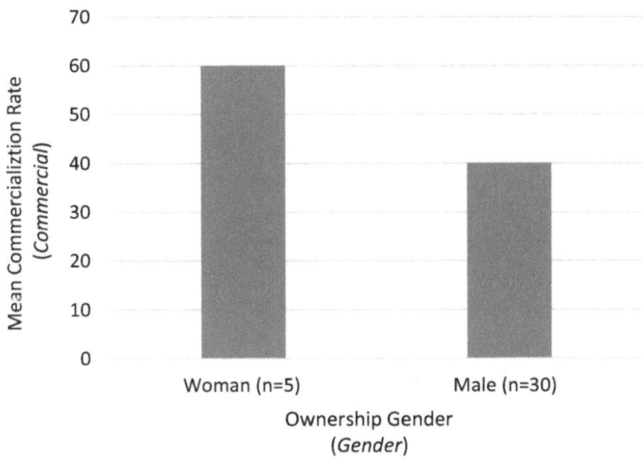

Fig. 6.4 Commercialization Rate by Ownership Gender (n = 35). *Source* NHLBI SBIR database

Table 6.1 Summary of *Licensing*, *Patenting*, *Publishing*, *Commercial* by Ownership Gender (n = 35)

Ownership	*Licensing (%)*	*Patenting*	*Publishing*	*Commercial (%)*
Female (n = 5)	60.0	0.20	6.00	60.0
Male (n = 30)	27.0	1.40	5.70	40.0

Source NHLBI SBIR database

metric in terms of the inflow of the stock of external human capital (HC_e) and external technical capital (TC_e) emanating from university relationships.

6.2 Knowledge Outflows by University Relationships

Unlike with ownership gender, there is no developed literature that has addressed the relationship between university-based human capital versus university-based technical capital in the development of Phase II technology, especially the knowledge outflow of Phase II technology that emanates from the funded firms. Treating university involvement as a homogeneous activity—meaning a university was involved in one undefined way or another—Link (2015) previously showed that university involvement per se was positively associated with the number of patents received from a Phase II technology using a large across-agency sample of Phase II SBIR projects. Link (2015) also showed that university involvement per se was negatively associated with the probability that the Phase II technology would be commercialized.

In Chap. 5, we suggested a knowledge production function as a framework for the study of the innovative behavior of firms that completed a Phase II SBIR project, and we hypothesized in Eq. (5.5) the following relationship between outflow innovation and external knowledge inflows. Equation (5.5) is reproduced here as Eq. (6.1).

$$I = \mathrm{f}(HC_e, TC_e) \tag{6.1}$$

where HC_e represents the inflow of an external stock of human capital to the Phase II project, and where TC_e represents the inflow of an external stock of technical capital to the Phase II project. The source of these external knowledge inflows considered in this chapter is a university.

The external human capital variable, HC_e, is dichotomous. It quantified whether or not the firm relied on human capital resources accessed from a university, *UniversityHC*. The external technical capital variable, TC_e, is also dichotomous. It measures if the firm relied on technical capital resources accessed from a university, *UniversityTC*. See the definitions of these two variables in Table 5.1, and descriptive statistics on these two variables were reported in Table 5.5 (n = 24).

The knowledge outflow innovation (I) variables considered herein are the same as previously considered in Chap. 5: *Licensing*, *Patenting*, *Publishing*, and *Commercial*.

Figures 6.5 through 6.8 illustrate the inflow of *UniversityHC* (n = 24), and Fig. 6.9 through 6.12 relate to the inflow of *UniversityTC* (n = 24). Two striking patterns from these figures are that *Licensing* (Fig. 6.5) and, to a lesser extent, *Publishing* (Fig. 6.7) are enhanced when the Phase II project engages with university faculty and graduate students (perhaps the latter relationship reflects that most faculty have publishing as part of their university reward structure). Generally speaking, *Patenting* is not enhanced through the use of university human capital (Fig. 6.6) but it is to a slight degree through the use of university technical capital in a Phase II

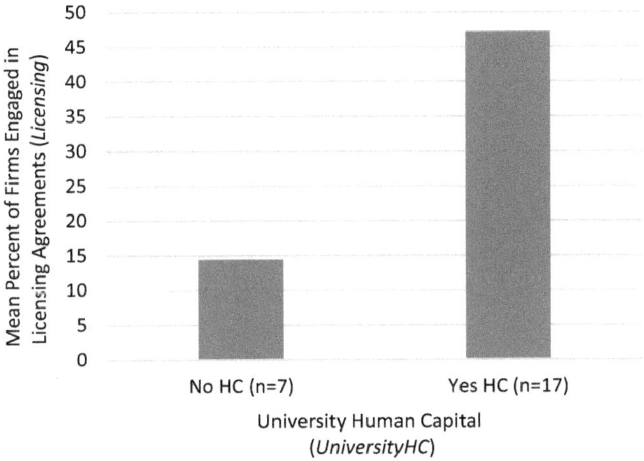

Fig. 6.5 Licensing Agreements by Use of University Human Capital (n = 24). *Source* NHLBI SBIR database

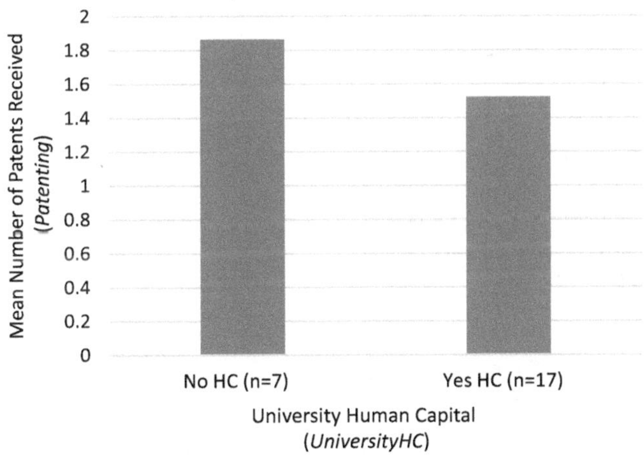

Fig. 6.6 Patents Received by Use of University Human Capital (n = 24). *Source* NHLBI SBIR database

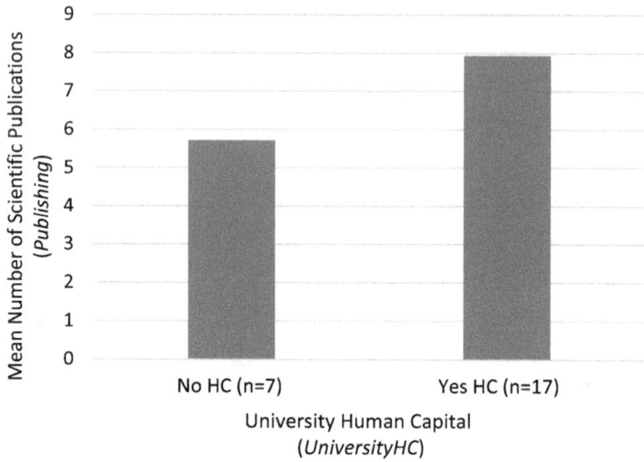

Fig. 6.7 Scientific Papers Published by Use of University Human Capital (n = 24). *Source* NHLBI SBIR database

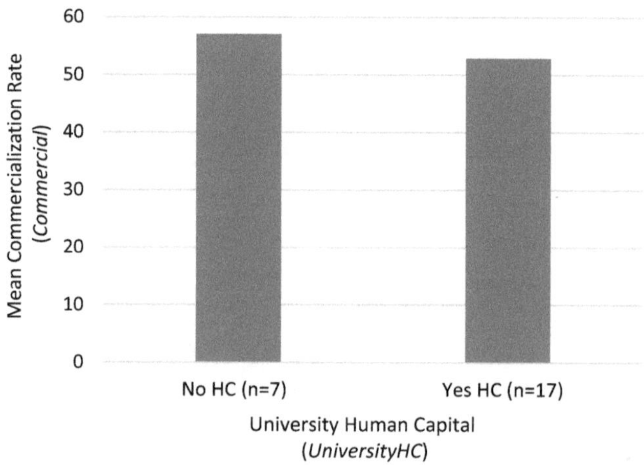

Fig. 6.8 Commercialization Rate by Use of University Human Capital (n = 24). *Source* NHLBI SBIR database

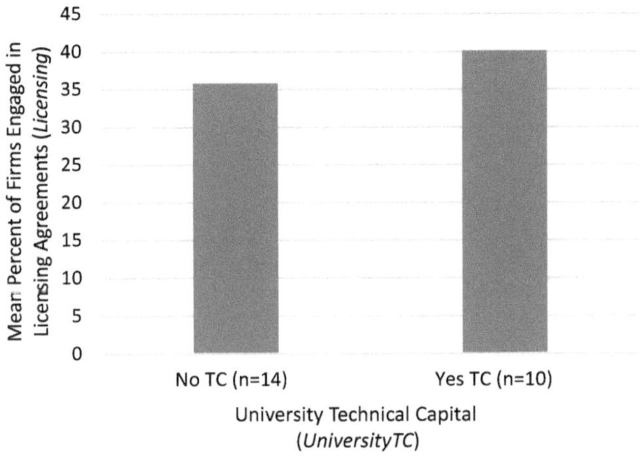

Fig. 6.9 Licensing Agreements by Use of University Technical Capital (n = 24). *Source* NHLBI SBIR database

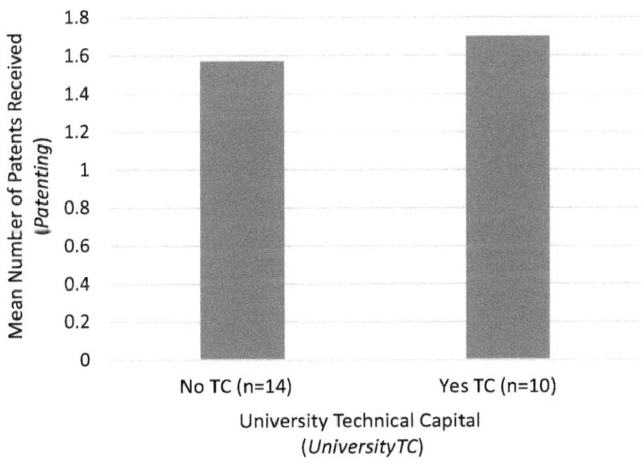

Fig. 6.10 Patents Received by Use of University Technical Capital (n = 24). *Source* NHLBI SBIR database

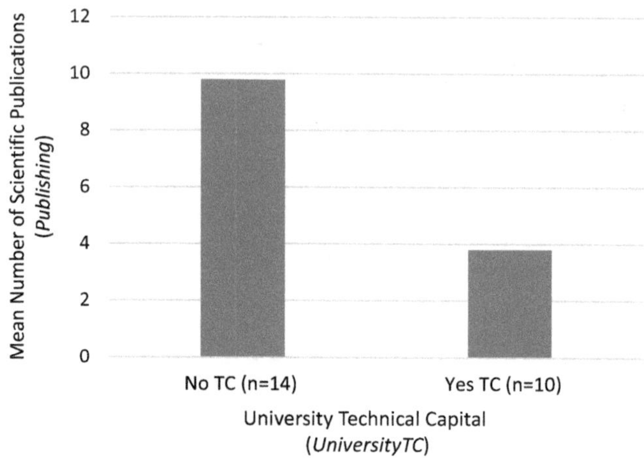

Fig. 6.11 Scientific Papers Published by Use of University Technical Capital (n = 24). *Source* NHLBI SBIR database

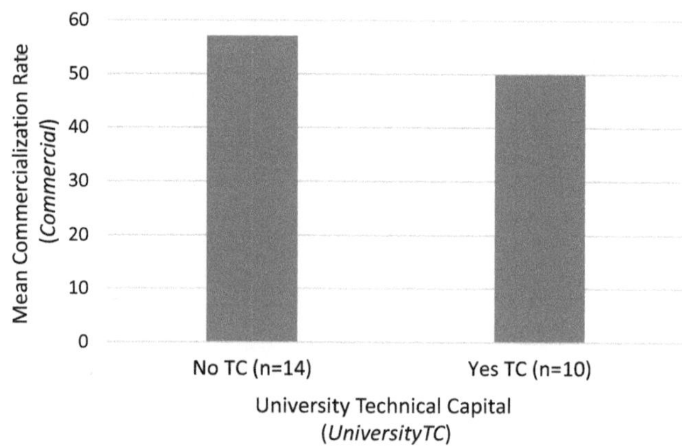

Fig. 6.12 Commercialization by Use of University Technical Capital (n = 24). *Source* NHLBI SBIR database

project (Fig. 6.10). *Publishing* (Fig. 6.11) is not enhanced through the use of university technical capital. Finally, university relationships in the form of human capital and technical capital do not appear to influence the probability of commercialization, *Commercial* (Figs. 6.8 and 6.12).

With more specificity (see Table 6.2):

- When either university human capital or university technical capital is used as a knowledge inflow to the firm conducting the NHLBI Phase II project, licensing agreements are, on average, greater. The mean use of licensing agreements is greater by more than 30 percentage points with the use of university human capital, but the mean use of licensing agreements is greater by just over 4 percentage points with the use of university technical capital. See Figs. 6.5 and 6.9.
- The mean number of patents received by the firm from its Phase II technology is less when university human capital is used as a knowledge inflow. But, the mean number of patents received by the firm is greater with the use of university technical capital. See Figs. 6.6 and 6.10. Recall from Table 5.3 that the overall mean number of patents received is just over 1 (n = 35).
- The mean number of scientific papers published related to the Phase II technology is greater by about 2 scientific publications with the use of university human capital. But the mean number of scientific papers published is lower with the use of university technical capital by about 6. See Figs. 6.7 and 6.11.
- The probability that the firm conducting the NHLBI Phase II project is more likely to commercialize from its Phase II technology

Table 6.2 Summary of *Licensing, Patenting, Publishing, Commercial* by Use of University Human Capital and Technical Capital (n = 24)

Categories	*Licensing (%)*	*Patenting*	*Publishing*	*Commercial (%)*
UniversityHC				
No HC (n = 7)	14.3	1.86	5.71	57.1
Yes HC (n = 17)	47.1	1.53	7.94	52.9
UniversityTC				
No TC (n = 14)	35.7	1.57	9.79	57.1
Yes TC (n = 10)	40.0	1.70	3.80	50.0

Source NHLBI SBIR database

in the absence of the use of either university-based human capital (lesser by about 4 percentage points) or technical capital (lesser by about 7 percentage points). See Figs. 6.8 and 6.12.

Table 6.2 presents a quantitative summary of these findings.

The following section describes the relationship between knowledge outflows and network relationships.

6.3 Knowledge Outflows and Network Relationships

Motivating this section of this chapter is the following observation (Moreno 1947, p. 268).

> Sociometric tests show in a dramatic and precise fashion that every group has beneath its superficial, tangible, readable structure an underlying intangible, invisible, unofficial structure, but one which is more real, alive and dynamic than the other.

According to Granovetter (1973, p. 1360), "Sociometry [is] the precursor to network analysis." And, Leyden and Link (2015) were among the early researchers to relate strong and weak network ties to the performance of entrepreneurial endeavors, such as research on Phase II SBIR projects.

If one thinks about the Phase II research process as involving the search for knowledge—external sources of knowledge in particular—in search area A_1 to start with, then the challenge for the firm conducting the Phase II research project is to identify relevant knowledge within that area and assess its relevance to its search objectives. Assessment, followed by exploitation, involves the perception of opportunity; but there is uncertainty associated with any action that is based on perception, and there is uncertainty about the relevance of such action on the desired realization of the search objectives. It follows that the realization of this firm's search objectives, that is the effective search performance, P, of the firm's identification of relevant new innovation related knowledge, will be a function of the characteristics of search area A_1, or any subsequent search areas, A_2 through A_i, as well as a function of the firm's internal effectiveness, γ, in identifying and exploiting identified knowledge.[1] Thus, for the ith search area:

$$P_i = \text{f}\ (A_i, \gamma) \tag{6.2}$$

Once in the search area, A_1, the firm must decide on search depth as well as search scope, both of which embody an element of uncertainty.

In this section, we explore two identified areas in which we assume the firm conducting the Phase II research project searched and then decided to exploit. The first area is related to other firms with which the research firm can enter into a marketing/distribution agreement. The second area is related to other firms with which the researching firm can enter into a research and development (R&D) agreement.[2] We arrive at this focused exploration in a rather ad hoc manner, yet from our perspective, it is a rather pragmatic way forward. As we reported in Table 5.5, these are the two most used relational sources of knowledge flows, that is of network relationships, exploited by the NHLBI SBIR-funded firms in our data sample of Phase II SBIR projects. And, the effectiveness, P, of the firm's identification of relevant new innovation-related knowledge from these two network relationships can be explored through the knowledge outflow metrics of licensing, patenting, publishing, and commercialization activity from earlier chapters that are associated with a Phase II SBIR research project.

Figures 6.13 through 6.16 show the mean *Licensing*, *Patenting*, *Publishing*, and *Commercial* behavior associated with Phase II research projects by the dichotomous extent to which the firm entered into or did not enter into marketing/distribution agreements (*Marketing*).

And, Figs. 6.17 through 6.20 show the mean *Licensing*, *Patenting*, *Publishing*, and *Commercial* behavior associated with Phase II SBIR

[1] Of course, the set of opportunities in search areas A_2 through A_i may be difference from each other. This concept thus implies that the effectiveness of a search, γ, should possibly have a time, t, subscript. We are assuming in this simple conceptual model that effectiveness does not vary across search areas, thus γ is not indexed. The symbols and discussion used in this model also came directly from in Leyden and Link (2015).

[2] The order of our listing and discussion of these two network relationships should not be interpreted to imply that a firm would first search for a marketing/distribution agreement and then a R&D agreement. We simply list these two relationships in the order that we presented them in Table 5.5, and the order in which we present them in Table 5.5 is the same order in which they were presented on the National Research Council (NRC) SBIR survey.

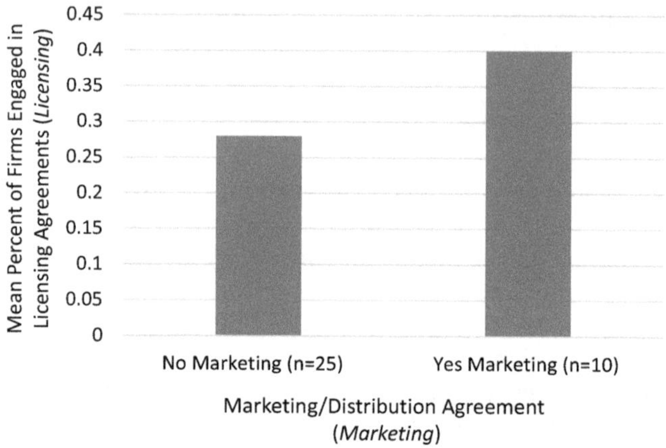

Fig. 6.13 Licensing Agreements by Marketing/Distribution Agreement Relationships (n = 35). *Source* NHLBI SBIR database

Table 6.3 Summary of *Licensing*, *Patenting*, *Publishing*, *Commercial* by Network Relationships (n = 35)

Network Relationship	*Licensing (%)*	*Patenting*	*Publishing*	*Commercial (%)*
Marketing/distribution agreement				
Not involved (n = 25)	28.0	0.96	4.00	36.0
Involved (n = 10)	40.0	1.90	10.1	60.0
R&D agreement				
Not involved (n = 28)	25.0	1.07	6.11	46.4
Involved (n = 7)	57.1	1.86	4.29	28.6

Source NHLBI SBIR database

research projects by the extent to which the firm entered into an R&D agreement (*R&D*).

The relationships shown in these eight figures are summarized in Table 6.3.

Specifically, involvement in a marketing/distribution agreement is associated with a measurable increase in licensing agreements (*Licensing*) associated with the Phase II project (Fig. 6.13) and in the likelihood that the technology from the Phase II SBIR project will be commercialized (*Commercial*) (Fig. 6.16). The mean percent of Phase II projects involved in a licensing agreement is 12 percentage points greater for projects involved in a marketing/distribution agreement compared to those that are not so involved, and the commercialization rate is 24 percentage points greater for similarly involved Phase II projects. See Table 6.3

Involvement in an R&D agreement is also positively associated with the mean percentage of Phase II projects involved in a licensing agreement (*Licensing*) (Fig. 6.17); and from Table 6.3, the involvement in a licensing agreement is 32 percentage points greater than for those firms not involved in an R&D agreement. However, the mean commercialization rate (*Commercial*) is not greater for firms involved in an R&D agreement compared to those not so involved (Fig. 6.20). This latter finding might reflect a timing issue; involvement in an R&D agreement might reflect that the firm first tried on its own to commercialize its Phase II technology but was unable to do so until additional research was done that was beyond the internal ability of the firm itself.

Regarding patenting (*Patenting*), the mean number of patents received is greater if the Phase II project was involved in a marketing/distribution agreement (Fig. 6.14) as well as in an R&D agreement (Fig. 6.18);

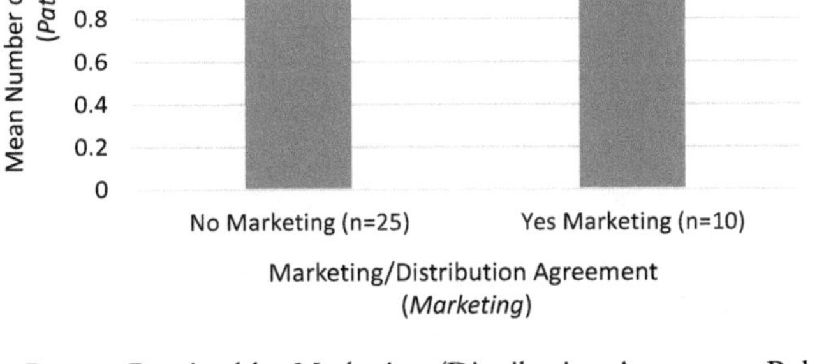

Fig. 6.14 Patents Received by Marketing/Distribution Agreement Relationships (n = 35). *Source* NHLBI SBIR database

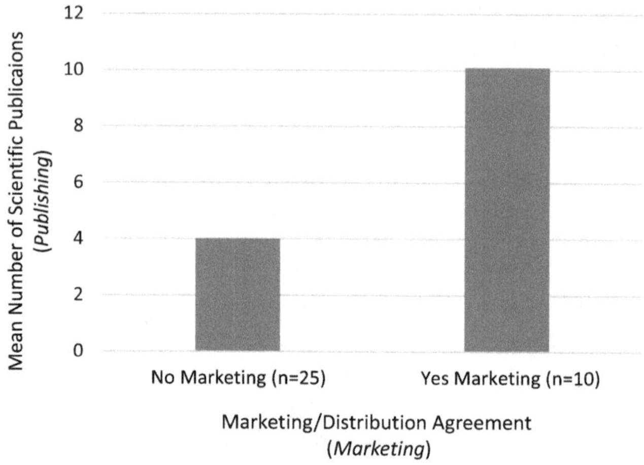

Fig. 6.15 Scientific Papers Published by Marketing/Distribution Agreement Relationships (n = 35). *Source* NHLBI SBIR database

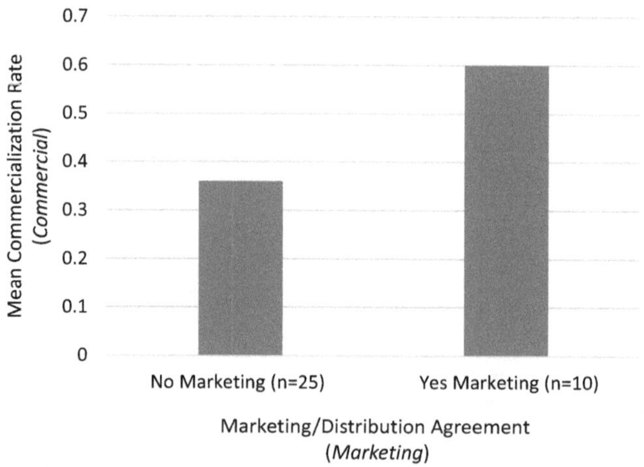

Fig. 6.16 Commercialization Rate by Marketing/Distribution Agreement Relationships (n = 35). *Source* NHLBI SBIR database

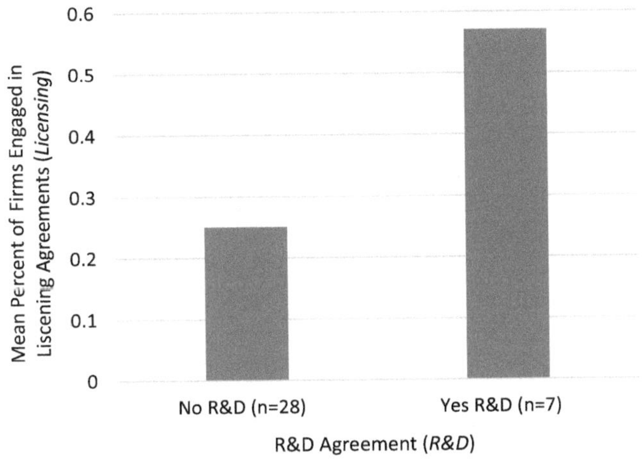

Fig. 6.17 Licensing Agreements by R&D Agreement Relationships (n = 35). *Source* NHLBI SBIR database

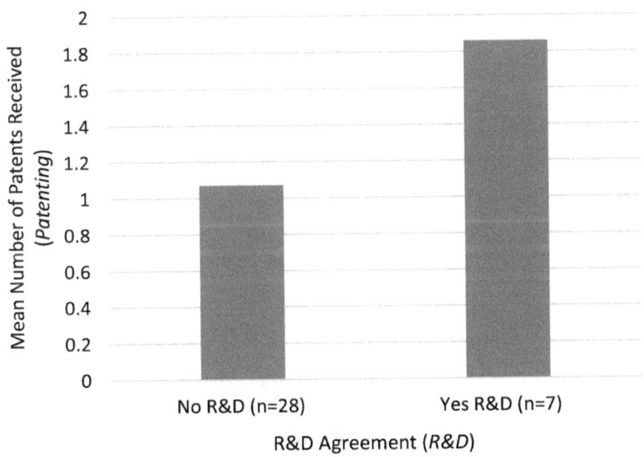

Fig. 6.18 Patents Received by R&D Agreement Relationships (n = 35). *Source* NHLBI SBIR database

respectively, 1.90 compared to 0.96 for involvement in a marketing/distribution agreement, and 1.86 compared to 1.07 for involvement in an R&D agreement. See Table 6.3.

Regarding publishing (*Publishing*), involvement in a marketing/distribution agreement is associated with an increase in the mean number of scientific publications (Fig. 6.15). In fact, such an agreement increases on average the number of scientific publications by more than 100%; from 4 scientific publications to 10.1 scientific publications. But, involvement in an R&D agreement is not positively related to an increase in the number of scientific publications (Fig. 6.19). See Table 6.3.

In the following Chap. 7, we explore the self-reported importance of SBIR funding on the firm's decision to pursue its current Phase II SBIR project. In other words, we ask a counterfactual question. Namely, we ask if the funded firm would have undertaken its current Phase II SBIR project in the absence of SBIR funding.

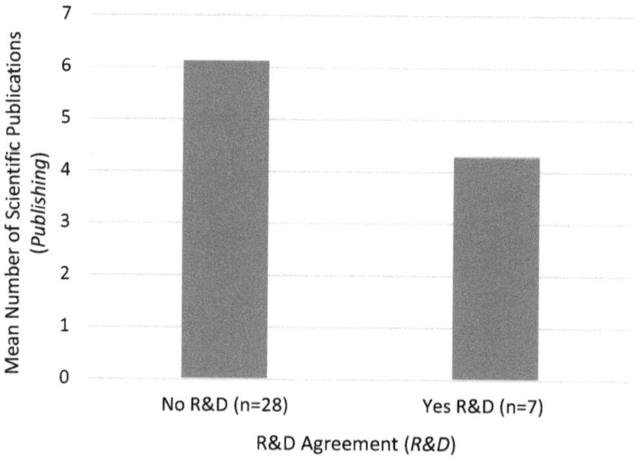

Fig. 6.19 Scientific Papers Published by R&D Agreement Relationships (n = 35). *Source* NHLBI SBIR database

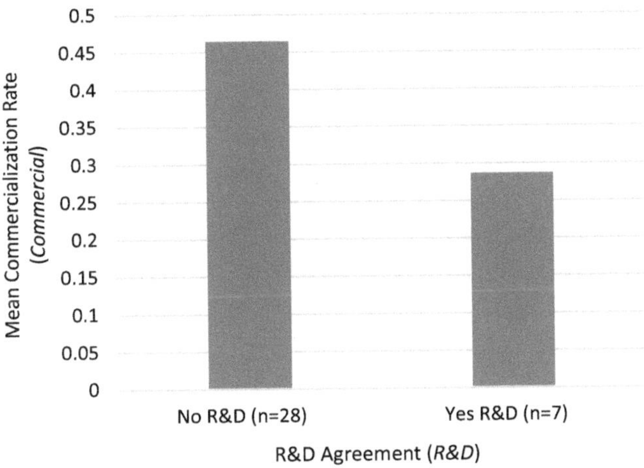

Fig. 6.20 Commercialization Rate by R&D Agreement Relationships (n = 35). *Source* NHLBI SBIR database

References

Granovetter, M. S. 1973. The strength of weak ties. *American Journal of Sociology* 78:1360–1380.

Leyden, D. P., and A. N. Link. 2015. *Public sector entrepreneurship: US technology and innovation policy*. New York: Oxford University Press.

Link, A. N., and L. T. R. Morrison. 2019. *Innovative activity in minority-owned and women-owned business: Evidence from the US Small Business Innovation Research program*. Cham, Switzerland: Springer.

Moreno, J. L. 1947. Progress and pitfalls in sociometric theory. *Sociometry* 10:268–272.

CHAPTER 7

Counterfactual Considerations

Abstract The counterfactual situation described in this chapter relates to the licensing, patenting, publishing, and commercialization activity of funded firms had they not received a Phase II award. The importance of understanding unanticipated policy consequences is given an historical context. Graphical and numerical probabilities of alternative scenarios are presented along with a discussion of the policy implications of the findings.

The discussion and analysis in the previous chapters of the book are based on the fact that the firm that proposed a Phase II project to the National Heart, Lung, and Blood Institute (NHLBI) Small Business Innovation Research (SBIR) program and received an SBIR award to undertake the research project, actually did undertake the Phase II project that the firm proposed. However, one might reasonably ask: What would have happened if the firm that proposed a Phase II project to the NHLBI SBIR program did not receive the SBIR award? To explore this counterfactual question, the National Research Council (NRC) SBIR survey included the following counterfactual question:

In your opinion, in the absence of this SBIR award, would your company have undertaken this project?
a. Definitely yes
b. Probably yes

A. N. Link, A. C. O'Connor, *The Economics of Heart Disease Research*, Palgrave Advances in the Economics of Innovation and Technology, https://doi.org/10.1007/978-3-032-13547-6_7

c. Uncertain
d. Probably not
e. Definitely not

Responses to this counterfactual question possibly offer some insight into the importance or economic value of the Phase II SBIR award to the firm and thus to society. The Phase II award is obviously of private value to the recipient firm because it covers the cost of the proposed research project to develop a Phase II technology. The Phase II award is possibly of greater and longer-term value to the recipient firm if developing the proposed technology enhances its research reputation. If the Phase II award was not of value to the firm, it would not have allocated internal resources to the proposal process. Even if the Phase II project fails, knowledge has still been created. Firms learn from false starts, and they learn what not to do in future research endeavors. But, the Phase II SBIR award likely only generates social value beyond the level of the firm if there is the creation of new knowledge followed by an associated outflow of the new knowledge in one of a number of firms.

One might reach the conclusion from Figs. 7.1 and 7.2 that that the eight firms that received a Phase II award and that responded on the NRC

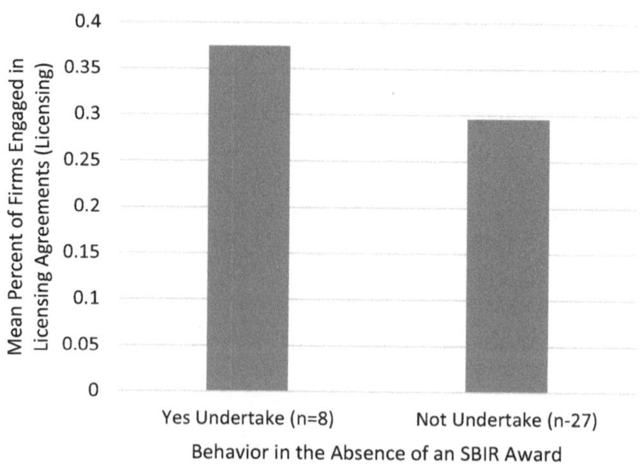

Fig. 7.1 Licensing Agreements Under a Counterfactual Scenario of Not Receiving a Phase II SBIR Award (n = 35). *Source* NHLBI SBIR database

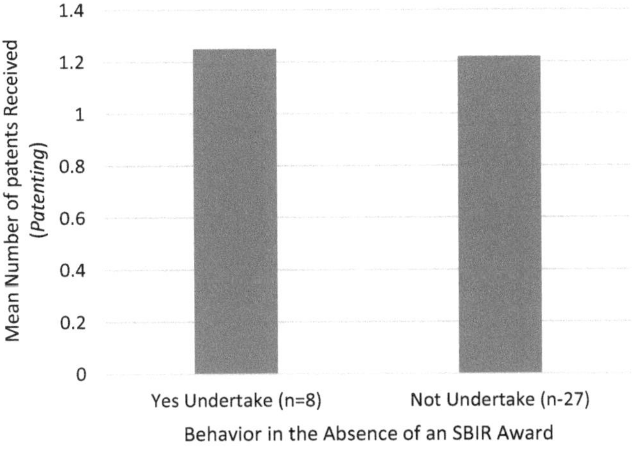

Fig. 7.2 Patents Received Under a Counterfactual Scenario of Not Receiving a Phase II SBIR Award (n = 35). *Source* NHLBI SBIR database

survey that they would have undertaken the Phase II project in the absence of SBIR funding (i.e., definitely would have or probably would have; noted as "Yes Undertake" in the figures) should not have been funded in the first place. To complement that conclusion, the mean percent of those 8 firm that engaged in licensing agreements is nearly 8 percentage point greater than the mean present of the 27 firms that required SBIR funding to pursue their Phase II project; 37.5% compared to 29.6%. And, these same 8 firms patented marginally more than the 27 firms that required SBIR funding; 1.25 patents compared to 1.22 patents. A reasonable explanation for the NHLBI SBIR program funding these eight firms is that there is uncertainty associated with any research project before the fact and even during the research process. Thus, those individuals within the NHLBI who make the final funding decision were likely acting rationally on observable information, and the firms' perception of uncertainly is not readily observable.

However, the pattern in Figs. 7.3 and 7.4, and the summary data in Table 7.1, allow for a retort. Those 27 firms that would not have undertaken the Phase II research project absent the SBIR funding were, on average, more involved in publishing; a mean of 6.5 scientific papers published compared to a mean of 3.5 scientific papers published for those firms that

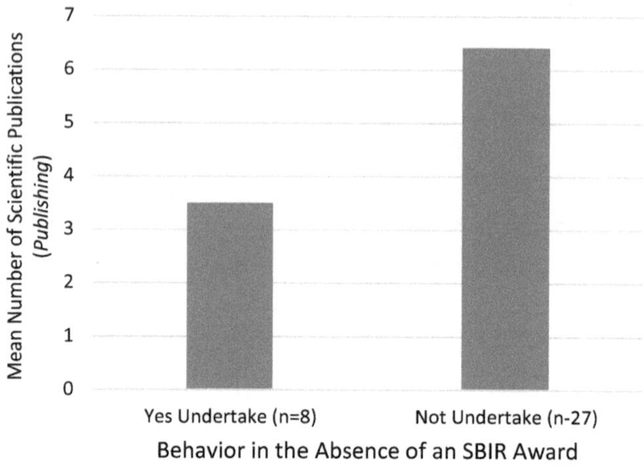

Fig. 7.3 Scientific Papers Published Under a Counterfactual Scenario of Not Receiving a Phase II SBIR Award (n = 35). *Source* NHLBI SBIR database

would have undertaken the Phase II project in the absence of SBIR funding. In addition, those 27 firms that would not have undertaken the Phase II research project absent SBIR were, on average, more successful in commercializing their developed technology; a 48.1 probability of commercialization compared to a 25.0 probability of commercialization. These latter two metric comparisons underscore aspects of the dimensions of the social value of the funded Phase II SBIR projects.

Alternatively, one might view the fact that there have been, and possibly will continue to be in the future, some Phase II-funded firms that would have undertaken Phase II research in the absence of SBIR funding. Perhaps one might refer to such a situation as an unanticipated consequence of public support of public sector support of private sector research.[1]

[1] Link and Van Hasselt (2023) have written about unanticipated consequences associated with the SBIR program, and they have traced the history of that concept to the 1848 writing of Bastiat (1995), and they have identified the modern version of unanticipated consequences to the writings of Merton (1936, p. 898): "The most obvious limitation to a correct anticipation of consequences of action is provided by the existing state of knowledge."

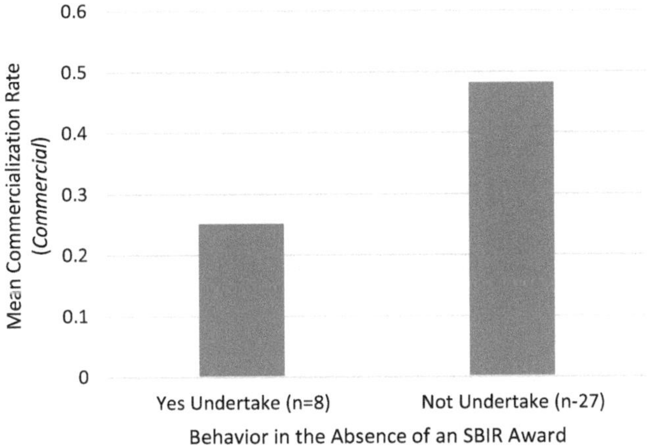

Fig. 7.4 Commercialization Rate Under a Counterfactual Scenario of Not Receiving a Phase II SBIR Award (n = 35). *Source* NHLBI SBIR database

Table 7.1 Summary of *Licensing*, *Patenting*, *Publishing*, *Commercial* under a Counterfactual Scenario of Not Receiving a Phase II Award (n = 35)

Counterfactual Scenario	*Licensing (%)*	*Patenting*	*Publishing*	*Commercial (%)*
Undertake Phase II project absent SBIR funding (n = 8)	37.5	1.25	3.50	25.0
Not undertake Phase II project absent SBIR funding (n = 27)	29.6	1.22	6.51	48.1

Source NHLBI SBIR database

In the concluding Chap. 8, the descriptive findings from the previous chapters are summarized. From that summary, we offer public policy considerations as well as a suggestive roadmap for future research related to Institutes in general and to NHLBI in particular.

References

Bastiat, F. (1995 original 1848) *Selected essays on political economy.* Translated by S. Cain and edited by G. B. de Huszar. Irvington-on-Hudson:Foundation for Economic Education.

Link, A. N., and M. Van Hasselt. 2023. *Small firms and US technology policy: Social benefits of the US Small Business Innovation Research program.* Cheltenham, UK and Northampton, MA, USA: Edward Elgar Publishing.

Merton, R. K. 1936. The unanticipated consequences of purposive social action. *American Sociological Review* 1:894–904.

CHAPTER 8

Summary Observations and Policy Suggestions to Enhance the NHLBI SBIR Program

Abstract This concluding chapter summarizes in tabular form the subject matter from the previous chapters and offers a research agenda that is applicable to the topics of each chapter. An inference from each summary statements is that Institute by Institute research is needed to understand fully the heterogeneity of research conducted at the National Institutes of Health (NIH) as well as the void of previous related work.

As we stated in Chap. 1, to the best of our knowledge, this is the first systematic effort to focus on NHLBI as an NIH Institute. Equally unique is our emphasis on scientific knowledge and innovative activity in small firms that was funded through the NHLBI small business programs. These motivations for this book are of course exemplified by the fact that heart disease is the leading cause of death in the United States. While the data that we used relates to a period nearly 25 years ago, we hope that our findings, summarized in Table 8.1, from the unique data that we had, will motivate Congressional inquiries into the funded research by the NHLBI through its SBIR program. Such a comparative study would allow policy-makers to better understand trends in the social importance of NHLBI research.

A. N. Link, A. C. O'Connor, *The Economics of Heart Disease Research*, Palgrave Advances in the Economics of Innovation and Technology, https://doi.org/10.1007/978-3-032-13547-6_8

Table 8.1 Summarizes the Subject Matter of the Previous Chaps. 2, 3, 4, 5, 6 and 7, and it Offers a Research Agenda that Applies to the Topic(s) of each Chapter

Chapter	*Summary*	*Suggested Future Research*
1	There are similarities as well as differences between the knowledge transfer metrics that are relevant to European country policy makers and technology transfer metrics that are relevant to the US policy makers.	Research is needed across countries on how knowledge transfer metrics and/or technology transfer metrics are used as policy yardstick.
2	Historical background on the National Heart, Lung, and Blood Institutes (NHLBI) is presented in this chapter along with a brief description of the Institutes within the National Institutes of Health (NIH). In addition to institutional information, comparative budget information is summarized for NIH and NHLBI. Funding trends over time are shown to be related to the Great Recession and to the COVID-19 pandemic. Much has been written about the US. Small Business Innovation Research (SBIR) and Small Business Technology Transfer (STTR) programs. In this chapter, the bones of the US. The SBIR and STTR programs are summarized. The organizational as well as Small Business Innovation Research (SBIR) funding structure of the National Heart, Lung, and Blood Institutes (NHLBI) is described. Also described are funding trends and award trends over time.	Research is needed to quantify from an econometric perspective the impact of aggregate economic events on NIH, NHLBI, and other Institutes' funding using US data as well as on impacts on health funding to agencies in other countries. Research is needed that compares across countries funding programs that support small technology-based firms. What little there is in the literature has been summarized in Link (2024b). Research is needed from an econometric perspective on the funding trends and award trends in this chapter. Research is also needed to estimate the relationship between funding and award trends and medical health breakthrough in subsequent years. Finally, research is needed on complementary resources that NIH, NHLBI, and other Institutes provide to support small firms.
3	The history of the NHLBI SBIR database is summarized. Selected data from the NHLBI database are described in this chapter such as number of Phase II awards by year and by geographical area of the United States. Also emphasized is that not all SBIR projects are successfully completed.	Research is needed, especially from an international perspective, on the institution history of similar data collection as well as on the research completion rates by sources of funding.

(continued)

Table 8.1 (continued)

Chapter	*Summary*	*Suggested Future Research*
4	A taxonomy of knowledge transfer metrics is offered in this chapter. The taxonomy includes metrics related to knowledge outflow metrics, knowledge inflow metrics, and two-way knowledge flow metrics. A point emphasized in the chapter is that knowledge flows are heterogeneous in nature. A knowledge production function is presented in this chapter. The knowledge outflow metrics considered are licenses, patents, publications, and commercialization rates. Associated with each are measures of internal human capital and internal technical capital. There is no consistent relationship among all possible pairings. The two consistent patterns that do exist are the decreasing relationship between licensing and firm size and the increasing relationship between publications and firm size.	Research is needed on the optimal portfolio of knowledge transfer mechanisms for firms. Research is also needed on the tacit versus codified nature of transferred knowledge and the resources that firms or organizations need to use transferred knowledge effectively. Finally, policy suggestions are needed, based on similar surveys for other countries, for additional survey questions of importance. Research is needed on the quality of knowledge outflow metrics. Patents, licenses, and publications are not homogeneous metrics, and each should be studied across all NIH Institutes in terms of their quality.
5	In an exploratory manner, the findings about women-owned firms and men-owned firms from the NHLBI Phase II SBIR projects are cautiously compared to the findings from portions of the extant literature. The economic impact of university-based human capital and university-based technical capital on knowledge outflow metrics is quantified in this chapter. This form of disaggregation of university resources on Phase II SBIR projects is unique to the academic and policy literatures. Two external network relationships are explored in this chapter:	Research is needed on a comparison of innovative output measures between minority owned small firms to non-minority owned small firms. And, the literature lacks a disaggregation of minority status (e.g., Black owners compared to Hispanic owners) in such studies. Research is needed on the role of universities on the research of small firms in general. Such studies should disaggregate university support in terms of human capital and technical, and the small firms should be privately funded and publicly funded.

(continued)

Table 8.1 (continued)

Chapter	*Summary*	*Suggested Future Research*
	involvement in a marketing/distribution agreement and involvement in a research and development (R&D) agreement. Such network relationships are related to the knowledge outflow metrics emphasized throughout the book.	Research is needed on the genesis of firms' network relationships. Are such relationships evidence of entrepreneurial insight? Are such relationships evidence of a purposeful offensive strategy or of a purposeful defensive strategy? Addressing such questions might be explored through case studies.
6	The data show that most, but not all, of the firms that were funded through the NHLBI SBIR program would not have pursued the Phase II research project in the absence of the funding. For some knowledge outflow metrics, those firms that reported on the National Research Council (NRC) survey that they would have pursued the Phase II research project in the absence of SBIR funding have outperformed those firms that required the funding in some dimensions but not all. Not all NHLBI SBIR funded firms successfully complete their Phase II projects, and for those that do not—failed projects—there information to suggest that the non-failed projects are more successful in generating certain knowledge outflow metrics.	Research is needed on unanticipated consequences associated with the NHLBI SBIR program and with other Institute SBIR programs. Very little has been documented empirically on this aspect of public support to small firms, and having a clearer understanding of such consequences might improve the SBIR program. Research is needed on Phase II SBIR projects that fail across all Institutes within the NIH as well as within firms publicly funded through other sources. Little is known about the reasons for funded project failure, and with such knowledge in hand failure might be averted in future projects.

Reference

Link, A. N. 2024b. The globalization of the US small business innovation research (SBIR) program. *Annals of Science and Technology Policy* 8:3–243.

Index

A.N. Link, A.C. O'Connor, *The Economics of Heart Disease Research*, Palgrave Advances in the Economics of Innovation and Technology, https://doi.org/10.1007/978-3-032-13547-6

FSC
www.fsc.org
MIX
Papier | Fördert
gute Waldnutzung
FSC® C083411

Kolibri 360 GmbH
Ferdinand-Jühlke-Straße 7
99095 Erfurt, Deutschland
produktsicherheit@kolibri360.de